A DEAN STREET MYSTERY
THE TV TERROR

'The winning episode features you escaping down a rope-ladder from a helicopter, landing on the roof of an express train and having a running fight with a masked arch-villain. And let's hope – for your sakes – that there are no more accidents.'

The chance of starring in a television programme about the exploits of the Dean Street Detectives is too exciting a challenge to be missed. But the young sleuths aren't on the set very long before they suspect that all is not quite as it appears to be. Events take a sinister turn . . .

Also by the same author, and available in Knight Books:

The Corridor of Ghosts
The Spying Machines
Fingers of Flame

The TV Terror

Bill Butler

KNIGHT BOOKS
Hodder and Stoughton

For
MARY
with all my love
BILL

Copyright © 1987 William Vivian Butler

First published by Knight Books 1987

British Library C.I.P.

Butler, William Vivian
 The t.v. terror.—(A Dean Street mystery)
 I. Title   II. Series
 823'.914[J]   PR6052.U875

ISBN 0-340-41118-X

The characters and situations in this book are entirely imaginary and bear no relation to any real person or actual happening

This book is sold subject to the condition that it shall not, by way of trade or otherwise, be lent, re-sold, hired out or otherwise circulated without the publisher's prior consent in any form of binding or cover other than that in which it is published and without a similar condition including this condition being imposed on the subsequent purchaser.

Printed and bound in Great Britain for Hodder and Stoughton Paperbacks, a division of Hodder and Stoughton Ltd., Mill Road, Dunton Green, Sevenoaks, Kent (Editorial Office: 47 Bedford Square, London WC1 3DP) by Richard Clay Ltd., Bungay, Suffolk. Photoset by Rowland Phototypesetting Ltd., Bury St Edmunds, Suffolk.

Contents

Meet the Dean Street Detectives   7
1. Fame at Last?   9
2. Flattering Questions   14
3. The Rough, Tough Tests   22
4. Spooky Kate   30
5. Schoolboy Sherlock   38
6. Dangerous Name   43
7. Gun and Games   47
8. The Big One   52
9. Exercise Rooftop   57
10. The Ideal Adventure   66
11. The Failing Crate   71
12. On With The Show   77
13. Steam Scene   83
14. 'No Risk This Time...'   89
15. Shake-up   94
16. Who's Doing It?   100
17. Another Little Accident   105
18. Very Intensive Care   110
19. A1 Emergency   117
20. Roof Chase – for Real   122

Meet The Dean Street Detectives

There are four of them, all aged twelve, all pupils at Dean Street Comprehensive School in the rough, tough town of Fenton – but very different from each other.

Anne Miller has long blonde hair and piercing blue eyes. She is impatient, impulsive, absolutely fearless – and impossibly bossy, according to her twin brother Peter. She has led the group through all their adventures – and into dead trouble more times than they can remember.

Peter Miller is also fair-haired, but his eyes are dreamy not piercing, and he always narrows them when deep in thought. He is the complete opposite of his sister, slow to act and by no means so fearless. But he has the sharpest eyes and ears, and the keenest detective brain, in the group.

Kate Murphy is the weirdo of the outfit. She's a battling Irish redhead with fiery green eyes and a temper to match. But she has a strange, haunted side, is terrified of anything creepy, and has uncanny hunches that often prove right.

Barry Bigley is the oldest of the Detectives – he's nearly thirteen. Tall, dark and slim, he is the toughest fighter in Dean Street Comprehensive, and likes to play it cool, modelling himself on such film stars as Roger Moore and saying everything in a mocking voice. Maybe he's a show-off – but there's a reason. He was once a fat boy, jeered at all day long – and he's determined that *he'll* do the laughing from now on!

Three of the Dean Street Detectives have police connections. Anne and Peter are the children of Detective Superintendent Miller, head of the Fenton CID, and Kate is the daughter of Detective Sergeant 'Spooky' Murphy of the Scotland Yard Murder Squad. When she was only three her parents were killed in a car crash and she was adopted by the Millers. She inherits her strange powers from 'Spooky'.

Detective Superintendent Miller does not approve of the young detectives. 'You'll get yourselves killed one of these days,' he keeps telling them. But that day has still not come – even though the group has tackled some of the most dangerous villains in the country: Mafia mobs, drug-smuggling gangs, even an international spy ring. They have been in tight corners over and over again – but somehow, thanks chiefly to their miraculous ability to team up together in an emergency, they've always *just* come through.

Now you've met the Dean Street Detectives, why not join them in their first holiday adventure – in which they become TV stars for a couple of days, but find stardom is no protection against . . . the TV terror!

1

Fame at Last?

The letter arrived at the start of breakfast, but nobody ate much once Anne had read it out. Dreams of fame and glory don't mix with cornflakes, and both Peter and Kate found themselves spluttering over every mouthful they tried to take.

'Read it again,' they both said as soon as they had thumped each other on the back and could speak.

'Yes, I'd like to hear it again, too,' said Mrs Miller.

'So would I,' said Detective Superintendent Miller ominously. He was the only one round the table who didn't seem excited at all. In fact, he sounded distinctly annoyed. 'Who did you say it comes from?'

'Britannia Television,' said Anne, and read from the envelope: 'Britannia Rules the Airwaves.'

'Oh, it does, does it? Then how come I've never heard of it?' Mr Miller barked. 'Must be one of the smaller companies, I suppose. Probably their programmes go out in somewhere like the Outer Hebrides.'

'Don't spoil it all for them,' Mrs Miller pleaded. 'Go on, Anne. Read the letter again.'

Anne managed a hasty gulp of coffee, nearly choked over even that, and then read:

'"To Miss Anne Miller, c/o Dean Street Comprehensive School, Fenton."' (The School secretary had obviously passed it on.) '"Dear Miss Miller: Britannia Television is launching a new series of one-hour weekly programmes to be called *Twenty-First Century People*. These programmes will feature children of remarkable achievement who seem likely to be leading Britons in the next century. We have decided to devote the whole of the first programme to the Dean Street Detectives, of whom I understand you are the leader. If you and the other Dean Street Detectives are willing to participate, and your parents also agree to your appearing on this programme, would you please ring my secretary at the above number as soon as possible? Our researcher, Miss Rosalie Penrose, would like to visit you and start things moving straight away. Yours sincerely, Philip Beatty, Senior Producer."'

There had been a stunned silence at the end of the first reading of the letter. This time, everyone began talking at once, including Anne herself.

'Think of it,' she said, her blue eyes blazing. 'A one-hour programme – all to ourselves! It's the biggest honour the Dean Street Detectives have ever had!'

Her brother Peter was, as always, beginning to see the snags in the situation. His eyes, as blue as Anne's, narrowed thoughtfully.

'Steady, dear sister. It isn't all that big a deal. The show is probably only for children. And it'll go out in the Britannia region, wherever that is, and I doubt if it'll be seen by anybody we know at all.'

'There you go – taking the fun out of everything as usual,' snorted Kate. She was Anne's and Peter's adopted sister. She had flaming red hair, wild, wide green eyes and what Anne and Peter thought of as the Irish habit of arguing about anything with anybody at the drop of a hat. 'Weren't you listening?' she shouted at Peter. 'These people are putting on a big new programme – a whole hour long – and they're going to devote the whole of the first one to US! Anne's right. It's the most exciting thing that's ever happened to us. It's got to mean fame at last!'

'Fame at last?' said Anne. 'We've already made headlines in the national papers several times over. They wouldn't be doing a programme about us if we weren't famous already. Still,' she admitted, not wishing to belittle anything her beloved Dean Street Detectives achieved, 'it will definitely make us more famous than ever.'

Detective Superintendent Miller had been listening to all this with deeper and deeper disgust. 'Oh, no it won't, young lady,' he said, rising abruptly from the table. 'For the simple reason that you have to get my permission to appear – and I haven't the slightest intention of giving it!'

The Dean Street Detectives' faces fell, their dreams of fresh glories vanishing as swiftly as popped balloons.

'Why not?' they chorused.

Mr Miller glared at them as though they were criminals about to be led away in handcuffs. 'Because,' he roared, 'I am simply not going to have my children paraded as freaks in front of the nation – or even a small part of the nation. Do I make myself clear?'

Anne could glower as menacingly as her father when she wanted to – and she did so now. 'Frankly, no, Dad, you're coming over distinctly foggily,' she said coldly. 'We're not going to be paraded as freaks. We're going to be treated as' – she read from the letter – '"children of remarkable achievement."'

'That's right!' yelled Kate. 'Not ordinary children: Twenty-First Century People!'

'Then that's when I'll give you permission to appear,' said Mr Miller heavily. 'Right at the beginning of the Twenty-First Century. And that'll still be a darn sight too soon! I've told you time and time again to cut out this detective rubbish. It interferes with your schoolwork. It stops you doing simple, ordinary things like making friends. It's so dangerous your mother and I hardly get a wink of sleep when you're on one of your stupid cases – it's a miracle you haven't been murdered a dozen times over! And what's more, it's making you more and more big-headed.'

Mrs Miller rushed to their defence. 'Oh, really,' she said. 'They're not *that* bad.'

'Yes, they are!' snapped Mr Miller. 'Just because they know how to take fingerprints and have been lucky enough to catch the odd villain or two, they think they're as brilliant as Sherlock Holmes, the Sweeney and the A Team rolled into one! If they go on this show, they'll become absolutely impossible. *And* they'll get more behind at school than ever – '

Even the mild Peter was getting a bit annoyed by this time. 'That'd be hard to do,' he said quietly, 'seeing that it's the beginning of the Easter hols.'

'That's right,' said Kate. 'We've got nothing in particular to do for three whole weeks.'

That was when Anne played her master-stroke. 'Unless,' she murmured, 'we do what Barry says, and start trying to track down the Fenton axe maniac.'

Barry Bigley was the only member of the team who wasn't in the Murphy-Miller household. The last time they'd seen him, he *had* suggested that they should tackle the axe maniac, but only jokingly, with his Roger Moore-style mocking grin. The case was one of the most dangerous in the history of the Fenton CID.

Mr Miller froze, and turned a shade paler. 'Listen, the three of you. I absolutely forbid you to have anything to do with the axe maniac business – anything *whatsoever*. Do you hear?'

Anne smiled sweetly. 'There's no need to worry, Dad. All you've got to do is give us the okay, and we'll be far too busy with the TV show to spare a moment for anything else. Won't we?'

There was a long silence, while father and daughter stared at each other, and Peter and Kate sat back, arms folded, waiting to see who would win. Not that the ever-shrewd Peter had much doubt.

Long before Mr Miller gruntingly, gloweringly gave his permission, he had winked at Kate and whispered:

'*Twenty-First Century People*, here we come!'

2

Flattering Questions

Ten minutes later, Detective Superintendent Miller had gone storming off to work, and Anne was busy on the telephone, with Peter and Kate standing behind her, interrupting and correcting everything she tried to say. First, she rang Barry Bigley to tell him the news. He was as excited as they were, but did his best to sound cool and bored.

'Well, well, well. So the TV world has got on to us at last. All I can say is – about time too. Where's the show going out, do you know? Hope it's peaktime on Sunday – nationwide.'

This was a bit much even for Peter. 'I'm afraid it's more likely to be lunchtime Tuesday in the Isle of Sheppey only,' he shouted into the receiver over Anne's shoulder.

'If we're all like Barry,' added Kate, 'Mr Miller's right! We *are* getting more and more big-headed every day . . .'

What happened next didn't make their heads any smaller.

Anne telephoned Mr Philip Beatty's secretary, and was told that Britannia Television would like to send the head of their Research Department, a Miss Rosalie Penrose, down to talk to them as soon as possible. The secretary asked for Anne's home address, and then said: 'Miss Penrose will be arriving at half past eleven.'

Miss Penrose arrived bang on time, driving up in a gleaming green Jaguar with a sticker saying 'Britannia Rules the Airwaves' all over the rear window. Miss Penrose looked as though she did quite a lot of ruling herself. She was a tall woman, with such a commanding manner that she might have been a headmistress – but a headmistress on Open Day, trying hard to be charming to everyone in sight.

'So you are the Dean Street Detectives,' she said, beaming at the four of them as though they were star pupils, stepping up to receive a prize. 'There's no need to introduce yourselves. I've been studying your photos on our files. You're Anne Miller, the leader, aren't you – my, you do have pretty hair. And you must be Peter, the schoolboy Sherlock – ah, yes, anyone can see you've got brains in that high forehead. And you're Kate, of course, the one with the paranormal powers. Mmmn, I can see that. My aunt is a clairvoyant, and she has green eyes just like yours. And you must be Barry – the hero type who always outwits the villain in the end – even when he's pointing a loaded gun!'

The Detectives were totally taken aback – except for Barry, who managed a mocking bow, and murmured modestly:

'Mind you – I *do* prefer it not to be loaded, but most villains aren't that obliging.'

Peter's eyes were narrowing. 'You seem to know an awful lot about us, Miss Penrose. Stuff that hasn't appeared in any paper I've seen –'

Miss Penrose smiled broadly. 'Good heavens, we don't rely on newspapers at Britannia Television! We've had a research team collecting facts about you for weeks. They've talked to old clients of yours, teachers on the staff of Dean Street Comprehensive, and a great many more besides.'

Anne was as impressed as Peter. 'Anyone would think you were doing a *This Is Your Life* on us,' she said.

Miss Penrose looked scornful. '*This Is Your Life?* That's done by another TV company entirely. We're far more thorough than that at Britannia!' She burrowed in an attaché case, and produced a thick file of papers. 'Now let me just check that I've got the main facts about you straight. Anne,

Peter and Kate — you've been amateur detectives for as long as you can remember. You were investigating crimes even when you were living at West Langham in Surrey, and were attending West Langham Middle School. Is that right?'

'That's right,' admitted an awed Anne, Peter and Kate.

'And,' added Barry, 'if your researchers haven't told you this already, the first crime they investigated was mine. I was at West Langham Middle School myself, and was known as the dreaded Bicycle Tyre Maniac.' He tried to keep his voice mocking, but it became hoarse and embarrassed. He didn't like remembering those days when he was a fat freak, bitterly angry with himself and all the world. 'No bicycle tyre was safe from me. I raided the bike shed, and let 'em down by the dozen. Until Peter here found an old bus ticket I'd dropped, and studied my Wellington-boot footprints, and pretty cleverly tracked me down.'*

Miss Penrose scribbled a note.

'Wellington-boot prints, eh? That's something I didn't have. But I think we know the rest of the story. Shortly after that, Barry, your parents moved to Fenton, and you started to attend Dean Street School. You were ashamed of yourself by that time, had slimmed down, and turned yourself into a tough gang-leader. Meanwhile, Peter's and Anne's father was made a Detective Superintendent, and put in charge of the Fenton CID. So you all found yourself at Dean Street School together — and teamed up to form the Dean Street Detectives. Shortly after that, you made the national headlines by beating a vicious heroin gang that was operating from the school itself. Then you tackled some bank raiders**; a Mafia mob called the Fortunos***; a gang of foreign agents**** —'

---

*The Voice from Nowhere **The Nightmare Clowns ***The Corridor of Ghosts   ****The Spying Machines

Anne started violently.

'That last case was top secret,' she said. 'How could you possibly have found out about it?'

But there seemed to be very little about the Dean Street Detectives that this Miss Penrose didn't know. The next minute, she was asking about their consulting room – a secret room in the disused part of the basement of Dean Street School, where they went during the lunch break to interview clients and hold conferences.

'That's really your headquarters, isn't it?' she said. 'I'd very much like to see it if I could – and I've a photographer waiting out in the car. If he could come as well, and take pictures –'

Anne frowned. 'The school's closed for the hols,' she pointed out.

'But there's a secret way into the basement we could use,' said Kate eagerly. 'It's a door with a broken lock that opens if you just give it a kick –'

Anne's frown deepened. She didn't think that made the Dean Street Detectives sound very dignified. And if they were caught showing strangers round the school . . .

The head of Britannia Television's Research Department seemed, on the other hand, to be delighted with the idea of sneaking in through a secret door, and wouldn't hear any arguments against it. 'Reminds me of my old school days,' she said. 'Midnight feasts in the dorm, and all that sort of thing . . .'

In five minutes, she had shot them round to the school in that gleaming green Jaguar, and the Dean Street Detectives were leading her and the photographer down the long corridor to the disused part of the basement. Dean Street Comprehensive was housed in an old, creepy building, and the Detectives' consulting room was in the oldest and creepiest part of it. The corridor became darker and dustier with every step they took. There were spiders and cockroaches everywhere, and now and again, they heard a scampering mouse or rat. Anne apologised, and said that the corridors were going to be swept clean next term. But the spookier the place got, the more pleased Miss Penrose seemed to be.

'What atmosphere!' she said. 'If only we could capture this on the show, we'd have every viewer thrilled to bits!'

Anne opened the door of the consulting room, and showed her in. It was a small room that had once been a pantry. High on one wall there still hung the old electric bells that had summoned servants to the HEADMASTER'S STUDY, THE DINING HALL and the other rooms whose names were displayed on dusty tags above the bells. The other things on the walls were more modern. On one of them, Anne had pinned press-cuttings from the *Sun* and *Daily Mail*, with headlines like TWELVE-YEAR-OLD SHERLOCKS BEAT KILLER GANG. There was a Scotland Yard Identikit Guide, contributed by Peter; an old Humphrey Bogart film poster, which belonged to Barry; and a photograph of Detective Sergeant 'Spooky' Murphy, put up by Kate. The furniture consisted of an old linen-chest, containing fingerprint powders, magnifying glasses and a microscope; two battered leather armchairs; a tape-recorder with a microphone, and a table with cans of Coke.

Miss Penrose and her photographer accepted a drink each, and then both of them got busy, Miss Penrose scribbling notes on everything in sight, and the photographer taking flashlight shots from every possible angle.

'Anyone would think,' whispered Barry to the others, 'that this was the tomb of Tutankhamen or something. It's the first time I've ever felt like a mummy.'

'Must make a change from feeling like a dummy,' said Kate, unkindly.

Peter was beginning to feel uneasy, without quite knowing why. 'What in the world are they playing at?' he wondered aloud. 'Surely they're not going to put all these photographs on TV? What sort of programme *is* this *Twenty-First Century People?*'

Miss Penrose's next remark left him even more puzzled.

'Right,' she said briskly. 'I think we've seen all we need to here. Now there's just one more thing I'd like you to show me. I've heard you had an exciting adventure last winter, being chased by a Mafia gang all over some slippery, snow-covered roofs. Could you take me up on one of those roofs?'

'Well,' said Anne. 'The most dangerous of them was the roof of the Bonetti detective agency, near Fenton station. If they gave permission –'

'Of course they'll give permission!' said Miss Penrose briskly. 'We're from Britannia TV!'

The agency was telephoned, and sure enough, permission was granted. Less than half an hour later, the Detectives found themselves leading Miss Penrose and her photographer through a skylight, on to a roof that was alarming even in the bright April sunlight. A small ledge, only a few metres square, surrounded the skylight. While standing on that, they were reasonably safe. But around them, tiles sloped steeply away in all directions, with nothing at the end of them except a strip of guttering and a terrifying drop to the street far below.

None of the Detectives could forget the last time they had been up here. A slippery, sleety rain had been falling, and it was pitch dark. In the room below was a vicious gang, smashing in the skylight and all set to give chase.*

'I can't imagine how you got away,' Miss Penrose said.

'Neither can we – now,' said Kate, shuddering as she looked around her.

'Yes, we can,' said Anne sharply. She never liked the Dean Street Detectives to appear stupid, under any circumstances. 'I'll tell you exactly what happened, Miss Penrose. We and

---

*The Corridor of Ghosts

the Bonettis – another group of young detectives who were with us – took it in turns to slide down those tiles, and then we grabbed hold of that chimney. The other side of that, there's only a short jump to the next roof.'

'Not all that short,' said Kate shakily. She remembered how she'd lost her balance, and fallen right over the edge. If Barry hadn't caught her, in the nick of time –

'Marvellous stuff, marvellous,' Miss Penrose was saying, writing busily in her notebook. 'We'll try and re-enact that chimney bit in the programme. A typical Dean Street Detectives adventure.' She turned to the photographer. 'Make sure you get a good shot of the chimney stack, Charlie. We'll want to build one just like it in the studio – oh, my God – '

She'd been so busy writing that she hadn't noticed where she was standing. Suddenly she'd missed her footing, and was sliding helplessly down the tiles.

Fortunately, Barry caught her arm, and with the help of the others, dragged her to safety.

'If there's one thing Barry's good at,' said Kate, 'it's catching people in the nick of time.'

'Practice, Katie me darling, practice,' Barry murmured modestly. 'Since there's no one in the world like you for falling off, and into everything –'

He broke off, noticing Miss Penrose's expression. Britannia TV's Head of Research didn't seem to like the Dean Street Detective style of humour. She had obviously been badly shaken by her narrow escape. Her face was scarlet, and suddenly she wasn't like a gushing headmistress, but a very bad-tempered one. 'I could have been killed!' she said, as though it was their fault.

'Oh, no, Miss Penrose, it wasn't as bad as that,' said Peter, trying to cheer her up. 'That chimney stack would have broken your fall, just as it did ours.'

Miss Penrose was definitely not cheered up. 'Don't you dare contradict me!' she barked. 'You're all the same, you so-called brilliant children. You're too clever for your own good. You just wait until we get you on the programme. Mr Beatty has a *way* with – with brats like you . . .'

The Dean Street Detectives just stared dumbly. All this was in such contrast to the flattery Miss Penrose had been dishing out before that it took their breath away.

Perhaps it was the dangerous roof they were standing on, with all its grim memories – but just for a moment, all four of them felt shivers down their spines.

It was the beginning – the first faint beginning – of the TV terror.

3

The Rough, Tough Tests

Back at ground level, Miss Penrose recovered, and tried to become her former flattering self.

'I'm sorry I snapped like that. It was rather a – an alarming experience, falling down those tiles. You must remember – not many people are lucky enough to have your nerves of steel.'

The Dean Street Detectives weren't fooled this time. Miss Penrose's mask had slipped. They knew what she really thought of them.

'Apparently,' drawled Barry, 'we're going to need nerves of ferro-concrete when we meet your producer.'

'That is,' said Anne coolly, '*if* we decide to come on your show.'

Miss Penrose was suddenly almost grovelling. 'Oh, don't pay any attention to what I said about Mr Beatty,' she gabbled. 'He's a very nice man, really, and very fond of children. It's just that –'

They had arrived beside her bright green Jaguar, which gave her a chance to break off and hastily change the subject. 'Hop in,' she said brightly. 'And I'll give you a lift home.'

Peter wasn't going to let her get off so easily. 'It's just what?' he said.

'Well . . . if you must know, Mr Beatty has a thing about phoneys and show-offs. A lot of them try and get on television, you know. He's determined that *Twenty-First Century*

People will ruthlessly expose anybody who's in any way a fake.'

There was an awkward pause.

'You mean,' said Peter, his eyes now narrowed to slits, 'he'll be aiming to expose *us*?'

'He'll be testing you, yes,' Miss Penrose said. 'In fact, he's arranged so many tests that it'll be like appearing on *The Krypton Factor*. But since you aren't phoneys or show-offs, or trying to fake anything, what have you got to worry about? You're *bound* to come through.'

She refused to disclose any more about these mysterious tests, and all through the drive home, kept saying how sure she was that they'd sail through them. The Dean Street Detectives didn't comment. They were getting more of those shivers down their spines every minute.

As soon as she'd dropped them outside the Millers' front gate, she said goodbye with a cheery wave.

'Your show is scheduled to be recorded Wednesday and Thursday,' were her final words. 'That's the day after tomorrow and the day after that. We'll be sending a car for you on Wednesday morning at 7.30 sharp. Don't be late. You'll make Mr Beatty *very* angry if you are. He's directing as well as producing the show. Well, I must be off now. Got a lot to do. We don't waste time at Britannia TV . . .'

And she drove off, her photographer, as usual, sitting silently beside her.

As the four stared after the vanishing car, Kate's green eyes glinted with fury. 'I vote,' she said, 'that we make Mr Beatty still more angry by refusing to appear on his rubbishy show. Testing us to see if we're phoneys indeed! *She's* a phoney if ever I saw one!' Her eyes widened, as they always did when she felt spooky. 'And anyhow, something about the whole set-up gives me the creeps.'

'Me, too,' said Peter. 'Whoever heard of a TV programme

inviting people to appear, and then going and putting them through a sort of third degree?'

Barry folded his arms, and put on one of his tough-guy expressions. 'You mean,' he said, 'you don't think you can take it?'

'Of course we *can* take it,' said Peter, although in fact he wasn't any too sure. 'I just don't see why we should have to.'

'I'll tell you why,' said Anne. 'It's because it's a challenge. And as long as I'm your leader, the Dean Street Detectives don't turn away from challenges! After all, we *would* be just fakes and phoneys if we funked appearing on a stupid television show!'

'Oh, Lord!' groaned Peter. He knew there was no holding his sister once she got into her 'fearless leader' mood.

Kate groaned too. The others had stopped feeling those icy shivers now, but she hadn't. She was more than ever sure that they were getting into something weird, sinister, dangerous. Both she and Peter had to admit, though, that this would be something quite new in adventures – and they weren't altogether sorry when Anne said, in her most ringing tones:

'So I say, when the car arrives on Wednesday morning – let's go!'

The car arrived dead on time, and whirled the Dean Street Detectives along a motorway heading north at top speed. They never discovered precisely what area Britannia TV served, but its studios were in a town called Kettlewell, which seemed to be a computer manufacturing centre.

This was a very different place from Fenton, with its miles of closed factories and empty warehouses. Here the buildings were all brand-new and gleaming. The Britannia TV headquarters – a near-skyscraper with more than twenty storeys –

looked as though it had come straight out of a science-fiction film. It was faced with sheets of mirror-glass, so that it reflected the blue of the sky and the green of the surrounding fields. But the glass was tinted, darkening everything it reflected. No sky was ever quite so sombre a blue, no fields were ever quite so grim a green. The effect was modern, even futuristic – but it was also just a little sinister.

The main doors were made of the same kind of glass, and the Dean Street Detectives were startled by their own dark reflections as they approached them.

'I look,' complained Barry, 'as if I hadn't had a bath for weeks.'

'For all we know, you probably haven't,' snapped Kate. She was feeling those shivers again, and wasn't in the best of tempers.

Once through the door, the four young detectives found themselves in a startlingly modern foyer. On the wall facing them was a huge painting of Britannia, complete with shield and trident. The shield was really an illuminated digital clock, surrounded by the words: 'Britannia – the NOW television station.' But the clock seemed to be out of order, and was flashing on and off, on and off, with longer and longer pauses between each 'on'.

'They ought to call it the NOW AND THEN television station,' Barry said.

'Oh, stop trying to be funny and let's get *on*,' said Anne.

She was beginning to catch Kate's nerves, and had to force herself to walk up to the reception desk. The girl behind it – a cold, superior-looking type – didn't even look up, until Anne announced: 'Good morning. We're the Dean Street Detectives.'

She woke up then – with a violent start. 'The Dean Street Detectives? Good heavens. They're all waiting for you in Studio One. Take the third lift on the right – to the eighteenth floor.'

The lift was as startling as everything else about this place. When they pressed the button, they didn't feel the slightest movement – and yet in less than a second, the doors slid open, and they were on the eighteenth floor. The producer's secretary was waiting to meet them, and led them through a maze of corridors, up to a pair of large swing doors. Above them were the words: STUDIO ONE. NO TALKING DURING TRANSMISSION.

'What's a transmission?' whispered Kate.

'That's when the show's broadcast, or recorded, of course,' Peter said.

'But if we don't talk during that, they won't have a programme.'

'It doesn't apply to us, stupid,' said Anne, adding proudly: 'We're the star performers.'

'Urghulck!' said Kate – a curious sound, produced by a curious feeling. The inside of her mouth had gone so dry that her tongue felt like a banana skin on a sand dune.

The next second, they were through the swing doors and were getting their first sight of Studio One. The place was enormous – about twice the size of Dean Street Comprehensive's assembly hall. Thick black curtains around the walls shut out all daylight, but the artificial light – from a battery of arc lamps covering the ceiling – was harsher, brighter and hotter than the April sunshine outside.

This strange, brilliant radiance revealed a busy scene. Sleek grey television cameras glided about everywhere, as silently as ghosts. Technicians in white overalls, looking oddly like hospital orderlies, moved around almost as silently, picking their way effortlessly across the mass of trailing wires on the carpetless concrete floor. Other people, mostly wearing sweaters and jeans and carrying clipboards, were standing around in small groups, chatting and smoking or drinking coffee. In one of the groups were two faces that were strangely familiar.

'That man there – I believe it's David Reynolds,' said Peter, in a hushed voice. 'You know – he runs that crime reporting programme, *TV Investigates*. And that woman beside him – I'm sure I've seen her somewhere –'

'You've seen her again and again, if you watch old movies,' the producer's secretary said. 'She's Bettina Rand. A big British star back in the nineteen fifties. Then she went to Hollywood, made half a dozen films, and has never been heard of since. Not over here, anyway. She's trying to make a come-back, and Mr Beatty has booked her to be the main presenter for the whole *Twenty-First Century People* series.'

'Will she be introducing *me*?' said Kate, her eyes wider than ever.

'Non-stop, probably,' the producer's secretary laughed. 'By the way, we've built some very special sets for your programme. We're going to use the one on the left to start with. Hope you approve.'

The Dean Street Detectives looked in the direction she'd indicated – and got one of the surprises of their lives. In that part of the studio, there was a small raised platform, which seemed to be the focal-point for all the cameras and at least half the lights in the place. There, under a positively blinding glare, was what looked like a small stage set, and the more they stared at it, the harder the Detectives found it to believe their eyes. In the middle of the set were two battered leather armchairs. Beside them was an old linen-chest. Next to that was a table with cans of Coke. On one wall was a poster featuring Humphrey Bogart; on another was a selection of Dean Street Detective press-cuttings; on another was a blown-up photograph of Detective Sergeant 'Spooky' Murphy. In other words, they were looking at a close reproduction of their own consulting-room. There was even a copy of the rusty bells on one wall, near the ceiling. And a door on the set stood half-open to reveal a dusty corridor, full of imitation spider's webs . . .

'Good grief!' breathed Anne. 'You've certainly gone to a lot of trouble to – to make us feel at home.'

'That is not *exactly* the idea,' said a harsh voice behind them. 'We simply wanted a dramatic setting for the tests we are going to set you. It is only fair to warn you that they'll be rough, tough tests . . . and we shall be televising every moment of them. So if you make fools of yourselves, millions of viewers will see you do it – because I can promise you, we won't be editing those moments out. But if you can't face up to that, you don't deserve to be Twenty-First Century People . . .'

The Dean Street Detectives whirled around. A tall, black-bearded man was standing behind them, his arms folded, laughing at them. He looked as sinister as any villain they had ever faced, and they had faced some very evil ones in their time. For a moment, they almost expected him to produce a revolver and tell them they were his prisoners.

But he didn't. He merely looked at his watch, and then barked at the secretary: 'We're behind time, Margaret. Get them into the make-up room, quick as you can. And warn them that if they want to suck lozenges, gargle, or go to the loo, they'd better do so now. They'll be on camera the moment they get back.'

His dark eyes glinted coldly. Somewhere in the depths of that beard, blinding white teeth flashed in a totally humourless smile. 'By the way, I haven't introduced myself. I'm Philip Beatty, your producer and director. And if you don't behave, I could wind up as your murderer before the end of the day.'

Presumably that was intended to be funny, but none of the Dean Street Detectives felt like laughing. Anne was too angry; Barry was too busy trying to think of a cool, mocking reply; Peter was too curious and Kate too scared. The last time they'd met somebody who looked and sounded like that, he *had* turned out to be a murderer . . . long before the end of the day.

4

Spooky Kate

In the make-up room, greasepaint was daubed very thinly all over their faces, their eyebrows were pencilled, and even the boys' mouths were reddened with a touch of lipstick. Barry objected particularly strongly to this, until Anne pointed out that Humphrey Bogart probably went through the same treatment before each day's filming. Kate was given a lot of special attention. Powder was used to hide her freckles, and lacquer had to be applied again and again before it subdued her unruly mop of flaming red hair. Some of the spray went into her eyes; a lot of the powder went into her mouth. She emerged coughing and spluttering and saying she was going to be sick.

'Violently sick,' she said. 'On camera. And all over that stinking ratbag Beatty. I'll make it a rough, tough test for *him* . . .'

Anne put on her sternest 'pull-yourself-together' expression. 'Don't be so silly!' she said. 'Tell yourself you're a Dean Street Detective and can't afford to have nerves.' Suddenly she made a rare admission. '"You're not afraid." That's what I say to myself when I'm scared. Under my breath, over and over again. It always works for me.'

'It would for you, O fearless leader,' murmured Barry, 'but it doesn't for ordinary mortals. If it's any consolation, Katie me darling, I'm trembling like a forestful of leaves. In fact, if you don't take my hand and hold me up, I don't think I'm going to make it back to the s-s-studio at all.'

It was an act, of course. Barry could stroll coolly through an earthquake. But he put on such a violent show of shaking that when he took Kate's hand, they both of them seemed to be doing some kind of flashdance routine. Kate burst out laughing, and suddenly felt all right again.

But at that moment, there was a tap on the door, and the producer's secretary put her head round it. 'Mr Beatty wants you all back in Studio One,' she said brightly. 'Which of you is Kate Murphy? Because she's in for an exciting time. She's going to be tested right away on her paranormal powers – by Miss Bettina Rand!'

Perhaps it was the powder covering her freckles, but Kate suddenly looked as white as a sheet, and seemed on the point of collapsing. It was Peter's turn to try a treatment. There was the spooky side of Kate and the battling Irish one. If he could make her come out fighting –

'Do you want Philip Ratbag Beatty to be *sure* you're a phoney?' he asked quietly.

That did it.

The light of battle returned abruptly to Kate's green eyes. In fact, it started blazing in them – and she actually led the way back through the swing doors of Studio One. The set had changed a bit while they'd been away. The leather armchairs were now facing each other. Bettina Rand was sitting in one of them, and Philip Beatty beckoned Kate imperiously to sit in the other.

'That's if you aren't too frightened to take the test,' he said, in a thick, sneering voice. 'You can always go home crying to Mummy and Daddy if you want to.'

Peter was beginning to be very puzzled. What sort of a producer was this Philip Beatty? He sounded as though he was almost daring them to appear on his show. It was a very strange way to get a programme on the air . . .

Bettina Rand, though, didn't seem surprised at all. She

invited Kate to come on to the set by patting the vacant armchair. When Kate arrived, she leant forward confidentially and said, in a soft, husky voice that had once thrilled moviegoers all over the world: 'You never want to worry about rude directors, darling. Take them in your stride. As I once said to Alfred Hitchcock himself: "You may scare the pants off the public, Hitch, but everything I'm wearing is staying right on me."'

Kate was almost too awed to smile. Now that she was sitting next to Bettina, she remembered all the times she'd seen her on television – mostly in old British movies, screened on Sunday afternoons. She'd seen her playing everything from a slinky female spy to a heroic WAAF in love with a Battle of Britain pilot. And she hadn't changed all that much. Her trade mark – shoulder-length jet black hair – was cut shorter now, but still showed no touch of grey. And she still had the same striking, instantly recognisable face, with high cheekbones, large pouting lips, and huge pleading eyes that looked at you as though you mattered more to her than anyone else in the world. Taking Kate's hand, she whispered: 'So chin up, darling. Let's take this Mr Beatty on together and show him just where he gets off.'

'No talking on the set!' roared Philip Beatty. 'Now listen carefully, Kate, and I'll explain exactly what's going to happen.' Now that he was being technical, he was no longer sneering, but sounded brisk and businesslike. 'First, we'll have a close-up of Bettina, who will introduce you as the Dean Street Detective who is *supposed*–' he stressed that word very heavily, and then repeated it ' – *supposed* to have strange powers. There shouldn't be any difficulty about that. Bettina will be reading the words off the autocue. That's that little screen beside the camera that tells you what to say.'

Kate nodded. She was getting so nervous now that it was hard to take in what he was saying. His figure was just a blur somewhere behind the blazing lights, but his voice came through sharp and clear, and terrifyingly urgent. She struggled fiercely to concentrate.

'While Bettina's describing your strange powers, Camera Two will zoom in, first on you and then on the photo of your father, 'Spooky' Murphy, which is on the wall behind you, just over your shoulder. We'll probably put creepy background music behind that bit. Are you following me so far?'

'Y-yes,' breathed Kate.

'Right. Then the camera will track back and we'll have a minute's chat between you and Bettina. At the end of that, Bettina will produce a large sealed envelope containing three drawings. My secretary will come on and blindfold you. Once you're blacked out, Bettina will take the drawings out of the envelope, one by one, and we'll see if you can say what they are. It'll be a kind of mind-reading act. Okay?'

Kate gasped.

'But – but I'm not a mind-reader –'

'What are you then?'

'I – I don't know, really,' said Kate. 'I – I just get hunches now and then.'

'Then we'll just have to hope that you have one now, won't we – or rather three of them, one after the other!' Beatty's voice was harsh and angry again. He gave Kate no chance to raise any more objections, but shouted: 'Right. Off we go, then!' and disappeared through a door labelled CONTROL ROOM.

The lights brightened even further, and became hard, white, terrifying. Bettina leant forward and gave Kate a broad wink, and a quick, reassuring pat on the hand. Then she turned to face the camera and started reading from the autocue, and Kate realised shakily that the recording was on.

'Welcome to *Twenty-First Century People*,' Bettina was purring in that famous husky voice. 'In this, the first programme in the series, we're turning the spotlight on that headline-making group of young crime-fighters . . .' Her words faded out as far as Kate was concerned. Her heart was pounding so loudly that it drowned them, except for an occasional phrase. 'And here with us in the studio is twelve-year-old Kate Murphy. Crime-fighting runs in Kate's family, but that's not the only talent she's inherited from her father, the late Detective Sergeant 'Spooky' Murphy of Scotland Yard's Murder Squad. Detective Sergeant Murphy was nicknamed 'Spooky' because of his uncanny powers . . .'

Kate saw one of the cameras glide forward, and realised that it was 'zooming in' on her – and the picture of her father over her shoulder. Creepy music surged through the studio – and she felt a sudden burst of pride. She hardly remembered being with her father in real life, but here they were together on television for just this one moment: 'Spooky' Murphy and his daughter, a double act at last. Suddenly she was nearly crying. She mustn't, mustn't, *mustn't* let her father down . . .

The creepy music faded. Bettina was no longer reading from the autocue. She was staring straight at her, those famous eyes seeming to stare right into her mind. 'I'm really rather *awed* at meeting someone with *real* second sight,' she purred. '*Do* tell me something about it, Kate.'

With waves of panic flooding through her, Kate realised that they were into the 'minute of chat', and that it was liable to be a minute of total silence. It wasn't just that her mouth was dry. Her brain seemed to have dried up too. All she could do was just stare blankly. Bettina's eyes became still more pleading. 'I understand you sometimes have strange feelings about the future – hunches, you call them,' she prompted. 'Can you describe one of those?'

'H-h-hunches?' said Kate faintly. For a moment, it was as though she'd never heard of such a thing in her life. But it was only for a moment. Suddenly something very odd happened. Perhaps thinking about her father had sparked it off; perhaps it was the blinding light and the atmosphere. For whatever reason, a change came over Kate, a change that Peter, Anne and Barry knew all too well.

'They shouldn't have asked her about hunches,' gasped Barry. 'Heaven help us, they've brought one on!'

Kate's eyes suddenly widened and rounded until they were almost like tiny moons, and they flashed with green fire. The next moment, she was out of her chair, and standing over Bettina Rand – which caused consternation amongst the camera crew, who had trouble keeping her in shot.

'I'm sorry to tell you this, Miss Rand,' she said hoarsely, 'but somehow I know that something terrible is going to happen. Something very frightening for everyone here today . . . including you –'

Bettina wasn't in the least taken aback. She was a professional, and knew just how to make the show go on. She stood up swiftly, and calmly eased Kate back into her chair.

'Well, thank you very much, Kate,' she said mildly. 'You've certainly given our programme an exciting start. And now,' she went on, turning and smiling at the camera, 'now that we've all seen the daughter of 'Spooky' Murphy in action, we're going to give her an opportunity to show you how powerful that second sight of hers really is. I have with me three drawings, in a sealed envelope. Britannia Television guarantees that Kate has not seen any of these drawings. I have no idea what they are myself. Now Kate is going to be blindfolded, and I am going to take the drawings out of the envelope, one by one . . .'

She broke off. Kate had bounded out of her chair again, her eyes still wide and wild. 'There's no need for all that!' she said crossly. 'I can tell you what they are right now. A windmill, a huge cat walking across a lawn that needs weeding, and – and –' Suddenly she was unsure of herself; perhaps the spooky mood was fading. 'And – er – a lamp-post, I think it is. Yes, a lamp-post on a seaside esplanade. Its light is shining on the waves –'

Bettina swallowed hard, waved back the producer's secretary who had been approaching with the blindfold, and tried hard to keep smiling at the camera. 'Yes. Well. It looks as though all I have to do is open the envelope, doesn't it?' she purred. 'It reminds me of all those times when I've been asked to present Oscars, and I can assure you, ladies and gentlemen, I'm just as nervous now as I was then . . .'

She didn't seem in the least nervous. It was obvious that she had come to the conclusion that Kate was just some kind of nutcase. She tore open the envelope, smiling broadly. Her smile wasn't so broad when she took out the first drawing, and held it out to the camera. It was very definitely a windmill; a rather sinister one, silhouetted against an evening sky. 'Very good, darling,' she breathed. 'But it *could* have been a lucky guess.'

She pulled out the second drawing, and her smile grew fainter still. It didn't show a cat walking through weeds, but a tiger prowling through a jungle, which was close enough to be pretty mysterious.

And when she pulled out the final picture, Bettina suddenly wasn't smiling at all. There was no seaside esplanade in it, no lamp-post, but there *was* a lighthouse, with *its beams shining brightly over a stormy sea* . . .

A gasp went all round the studio. Bettina still proved equal to the occasion. 'Well, Kate, you've certainly proved you've got powers all right,' she said, smiling. Turning to the camera again, she ended the interview with a dramatic question. 'What do you think, viewers? Does this mean that something very frightening *is* going to happen to all of us here today? I tell you frankly – I'm shivering in my shoes . . .'

She smiled and bowed. The cameras stopped whirring, and Philip Beatty came storming out of the control room. 'What a mess!' he roared at Kate. 'You stupid kid! You didn't do a *thing* you were told . . .'

Bettina rushed to Kate's rescue. 'But surely, it was *marvel-*

lous television, darling,' she told Beatty. 'And you can't deny she passed the test.'

Philip Beatty glowered. It was exactly as though that was what was annoying him – the thought that one of the Dean Street Detectives had actually not turned out to be a phoney. 'We'll see what the next one's made of,' he barked. 'Get the set ready for the Schoolboy Sherlock segment.'

Peter tensed. He supposed that meant that they were going to start on him. It was his turn to feel his throat going dry – and it didn't exactly help when Kate came over to join him, Anne and Barry. She was still in her spookiest mood.

'Do be careful, Peter,' she said. 'This frightening thing that's going to happen . . . In some way, I know it's going to start *through you*!'

5

Schoolboy Sherlock

'Thanks very much,' said Peter. 'That's all I need! Thank the Lord I've been hearing about your hunches all my life – and can remember a few million of them that *didn't* come true.'

Maybe it wasn't the kindest thing to say, but after all, Kate didn't need treating gently now. 'If anyone does,' he told himself grimly, 'it's *me*!'

Whenever things looked like getting tough, and he was always the first to spot trouble coming, Peter's natural instinct was to turn and run. And at the moment, that instinct was telling him to run a mile.

Very alarming things were happening down on the set. Bettina Rand had gone. Various objects – a chart, and something long and thin that looked like a walking-stick – were being brought on. David Reynolds, the presenter from *TV Investigates*, was walking towards the interviewer's armchair. Peter was a fan of *TV Investigates*, and had seen Reynolds many times. A burly man with a bulldog face, made even tougher-looking by large square spectacles, he was the sort of interviewer who showed no mercy to anyone. Peter had even watched him tearing the Chief Commissioner of Scotland Yard to shreds . . .

Reynolds sat down heavily, and glared round the studio until his massive spectacles focussed on Peter. 'Right, lad,' he called out. 'Come up here, and let's see what sort of stuff you're made of.'

Peter tried to accept the invitation, but it seemed as

though his legs had other ideas. They simply refused to obey his command to move, until Anne helped him on his way with a surprise thump on the back and a sharp: 'Get going, for Heaven's sake! Do you want to make a complete idiot of yourself?'

The mild Peter for once was stung into making quite a sharp reply. 'No, dear sister. I usually leave that sort of thing to you,' he said.

He was grateful to Anne for one thing, anyway. She'd got him moving, and now that he'd started walking, he couldn't stop. As though in a dream — which felt more like a walking nightmare — he found himself striding across the studio, and next moment, was blinking stupidly under the bright lights of the set. He looked dazed, confused and hardly aware of what he was doing. But in fact, his sharp eyes and ears missed nothing that was going on in the studio. He could even hear Philip Beatty whispering softly to his secretary: 'This one's a sitting duck. Reynolds is going to make mincemeat of him.' He sounded really pleased. Once again, Peter found himself wondering what sort of a producer this Beatty was . . .

Not that he had time to wonder about anything for long.

His spectacles catching the light and flashing like the eyes of some alien monster, Reynolds was commanding: 'Right, then, lad, you come and sit by me.'

Peter swallowed hard. It was an enormous swallow, that seemed to reach right down into his stomach and scoop up some of the butterflies fluttering there. Then, feeling every bit as dazed and stupid as he looked, he sat down in the other armchair.

'Okay, Peter, or whatever your name is,' came Philip Beatty's voice from the studio floor. 'What's going to happen is very simple. David Reynolds here is going to introduce you, reading from the autocue. Then you're going to be set two quick tests. First, we want you to decode a three-word message. Then you'll be asked to decide how a murder was committed. You'll have to be very quick, I'm afraid. This part of the programme should only take two minutes. So David can't allow you more than a maximum of ten seconds for each part of the test.'

To Peter's surprise, it was Reynolds who started making objections. His bushy eyebrows shot up until there was a good half-inch between them and the rims of those ferocious square spectacles.

'Ten seconds?' he barked. 'The boy would have to be a flaming genius to do tricky tests in that!'

'Precisely!' said Philip Beatty. 'And if he isn't a flaming genius, he has no place in this show. Off we go, then.' As before, he disappeared into the control room. The lights changed from dazzling to blinding. And as the cameras moved in, David Reynolds began reading from the autocue.

'And now I have with me Peter Miller, the Dean Street Detective, so brilliant that he is said to be like a schoolboy Sherlock Holmes. And to begin with, we're setting him a test that the great Sherlock himself would appreciate: three words to be decoded.' Reynolds waved a hand. An assistant came forward, and started to do something to a chart on the wall behind Peter's head.

Reynolds, meanwhile, began the interview proper.

'Hullo, Peter,' he said.

'Um. Well. Hullo,' said Peter. He was screwing up his face, narrowing his eyes against the light, and looking as unlike a brilliant schoolboy Sherlock as anyone could be.

'You all ready?' Reynolds asked doubtfully.

'Oh. Er. Yes. Sure,' Peter grunted.

'Right, then. In a moment I'm going to ask you to turn round. Behind your back you'll see three words, which you have to decode while I count ten. That's not a lot of time, but I'm sure you'll do your best.'

'Oh. Right. Yes. Well. I will,' said Peter stupidly.

'Then turn round – now.'

Peter turned, and saw that the words were:
GHDQ VWUHHW GHWHFWLYHV

This came as no surprise to him at all. For several seconds, he had been seeing them reflected in David Reynolds's spectacles, and he had always been good at reading looking-glass writing. As a matter of fact, he had been trying hard *not* to look at them, because that would really have been cheating. It was a relief to be able to stare at them openly, and get to work.

The best way to start decoding, he remembered, was always to notice the letter that occurred most often, because that would most likely turn out to be an 'E'. In these words, the letter occurring most often was 'H'. If 'E' had become 'H', then each letter of the alphabet had been moved three places along. It took Peter's agile brain no time at all to work out what that meant. 'D' had become 'G', 'A' had become 'D', 'N' had become 'Q' ... and GHDQ VWUHHW GHWHFWLYHV had originally been –

'Dean Street Detectives,' he said aloud, and couldn't understand why David Reynolds was staring at him so oddly.

The tough presenter had just opened his mouth to say –
'*Four*'.

Not looking nearly so tough now, he picked up the long, thin object and held it out. It *was* a walking-stick, Peter realised, with a massive carved-wood handle, shaped like a fox's head.

'Now we want you to make a deduction,' David Reynolds said. 'This object has been supplied to us by the Black Museum at Scotland Yard. Back at the turn of the century, it was found lying in the road beside the corpse of a murdered man. How would you say the murder had been committed?'

Peter leant back in the chair, and began twirling the stick in his hands. Now that he had more confidence, he was beginning to look just a little like a schoolboy Sherlock at last.

'Take your time,' Reynolds said calmly. 'I should warn you, this is a trick question, and not a very easy one. Since you decoded those words so rapidly, I can give you a full fifteen seconds to answer this time. Fifteen seconds – starting – oh.'

There was no point in saying 'now'.

Peter had given the fox's head a sharp twist. The rest of the walking stick had fallen away, leaving a gleaming, rapier-like blade. 'I think that's what they used to call a swizzle-stick,' he murmured. 'I've often heard about them, but never seen one. So the murder must have been a stabbing – wouldn't you say?'

David Reynolds had to fill in the rest of the two minutes with chat. At the end of it, Philip Beatty emerged from the control room to shout: 'Take ten minutes' break, everyone. Just ten minutes, mind, not a second more!' His face was as sour as though he'd bitten on a dozen lemons, one after the other.

'There goes a man,' drawled Barry to Anne and Kate, 'who's feeling well and truly swizzled.'

Anne burst out laughing. Kate didn't. She'd noticed that Peter was suddenly nowhere to be seen. And for some reason she couldn't explain, she found that – frightening . . .

6

Dangerous Name

At that moment, Peter was, in fact, in a little disused office leading off the studio: a small bare room, with nothing in it but a desk and a couple of chairs. Immediately the ten-minute break had started, David Reynolds had seized Peter's arm, and pulled him in there.

'Just want a quick word with you, if you can spare a moment.'

'Er. Well. Yes, of course,' Peter had said, in his usual confused way.

He'd noticed that something odd had come over the tough TV investigator. David Reynolds's massive frame was shaking all over, and his huge pair of spectacles had slid almost comically far down his sweaty, slippery nose. Reynolds realised this himself, and jerked them up again sharply before peering at Peter very hard indeed.

'You don't fool me with that vague style of yours, son. You may look like some kind of idiot, but you're actually as sharp as they come. That test was so loaded against you that I was ashamed to be part of it. But you showed us all up, and I'm glad you did. Now listen.' He was still holding the clipboard he had been using as an interviewer, and glanced down at it quickly. 'I've a note here that says you're the son of Detective Superintendent Miller of the CID. Is that right?' Peter nodded. 'Good. I've heard of your father – he did some remarkable things when he was with the Murder Squad some years ago. I think maybe that both you and he can help me.'

Peter was so startled that for once he came straight to the point, without any 'Ers' or 'Wells'.

'How?' he asked.

Reynolds sat down heavily on the little room's only desk. 'I'm in a spot,' he said. 'I'm like the Dean Street Detectives in a way. I can't stop investigating, even when it's not my business to do so. And recently I've been investigating someone who's turned out to be very dangerous indeed. There have been so many attempts on my life that I'm scared – very scared, as you can see.'

Peter's eyes narrowed. 'This someone,' he said. 'Would he – or she – be connected with this programme?'

Reynolds began to nod, then changed his mind, and turned it into a shrug. 'The less you know, the better it would be for your health,' he said. 'At least – while you and your friends are on the show.'

'Then how can we possibly help you?' Peter asked.

'Like this,' Reynolds said.

There was a pencil attached to the clipboard. He took it and began scribbling something on the top sheet. 'If anything should happen to me, I want you to get on to your father, and show him this name – what's the matter?'

Peter had suddenly tensed. He had thought he'd heard footsteps, very stealthy footsteps, just outside the door.

David Reynolds had praised Peter for being sharp, but it was obvious that he didn't miss much himself. 'Someone listening, you reckon?' he whispered, so softly that Peter had almost to lip-read the words.

Peter nodded, and within a split second, moving astonishingly fast for such a big man, TV's top crime investigator was over by the door, and hurling it open.

There was nobody outside – at least, nobody *immediately* outside. The door gave directly on to Studio One, and a large number of people were milling around there, of course. Philip Beatty, his secretary Margaret, Bettina Rand, a few dozen technicians, Anne, Barry and Kate – they were none of them very far away. And Peter noticed, incidentally, another familiar face on the scene: Miss Rosalie Penrose, the head of Britannia TV's research department, was walking across to Philip Beatty, beaming round her with the 'headmistress-at-a-prizegiving' air that seemed to be her public face. Just about any of them, Peter reasoned, *could* have been the eavesdropper outside the door. Of course, he, or she, couldn't have been exactly pressing an ear to it, or looking through the keyhole, just pretending to be casually strolling by . . .

Reynolds was sweating so much now that his spectacles were partly steamed-up. He pulled Peter back into the room, and closed the door firmly behind him. 'I've changed my mind, son,' he said shakily. 'It's not fair of me to get a kid mixed up in a thing like this.' He had left the clipboard lying on the desk. He rushed across to it, and ripping off the top sheet, screwed it up fiercely and stuffed it into the back pocket of his trousers. 'Forget we ever had this little chat. And forget all about this name. It's far too dangerous for an adult, let alone a kid, to know. And I can only hope and pray that the person concerned *doesn't think I've told it to you already* . . .'

He opened the door again, and took one more nervous look around the studio. The ten-minute break was over now. Philip Beatty was shouting to the technicians to start getting the set ready for the next part of the show, the Barry Bigley test. 'Remember, this is quite different from anything that's been tried on TV before,' he was barking. 'If we're not careful, somebody could get hurt.' He sounded as if he was hoping it would be Barry.

Peter heard all this over David Reynolds's shoulder, but he wasn't giving it his full attention. He was far more interested in that clipboard, which was still on the desk-top. Reynolds had ripped off the top sheet, but he had been using a sharp pencil, which should have left a deep impression on the sheet underneath. If he could manage to pocket that, thought Peter, and tried some fingerprint powder on it when he got home, maybe he'd be able to bring up at least part of what had been written. If he could see even a few letters of that dangerous name . . .

Always bad at acting quickly, Peter ripped at the sheet so clumsily that the clipboard clattered on to the floor. Reynolds swung round as fast as though a bomb had exploded behind him. 'What are you playing at, son? I hope to God you've not been trying to read what I've just written. Give me that clipboard – now.'

'Yes. Well. Right. At once,' Peter mumbled.

He picked up the clipboard, and handed it over, dropping it twice in the process. This time, he was deliberately being clumsy. He was trying to cover up the fact that all the while he was busily slipping that second sheet into his own back pocket.

With, he hoped, the name that was so dangerous to know . . .

7

Gun and Games

'Where were you?' demanded Kate, as Peter walked across the studio back to the group. 'And what happened? Something frightening?'

'Well – yes and no,' said Peter cautiously. He always loathed admitting that a hunch of Kate's had proved right. But, in all honesty, he had to add: 'But mostly yes.'

He described the conversation he'd had with David Reynolds, and the footsteps outside. 'Did any of you see who was standing there?' he asked. 'You were all in full view of the door, the whole time.'

'True enough,' said Anne. 'But as we'd no idea you were in there, none of us was exactly giving it the eagle eye.' She frowned. 'Mind you, Miss Penrose did pause over there on her way in just now.'

'Yes,' said Kate brightly. 'Philip Beatty strolled over there, too, when he was drinking his coffee. So did his secretary. *And* Bettina Rand –'

'So we're not exactly short of suspects, are we?' drawled Barry. 'This is turning into a real Agatha Christie situation. Anybody or everybody could have been outside that door. I think myself – oh, sorry, folks. It's time for me to stop thinking, and start panicking!'

Philip Beatty was staring straight at him, and barking imperiously. 'Okay, Barry. Come up on to the set, please.' His teeth flashed in that curious half-dazzling, half-leering smile. 'Miss Penrose tells me you're the tough hero type.

So we've organised something really heroic to put you through.'

'How very kind of you, Mr Beatty, sir,' said Barry, mockingly.

Beatty stared. He didn't like the idea of a Dean Street Detective making fun of him, not one little bit. 'You may not think me so kind by the time it's finished,' he snapped, and disappeared into the control room, without stopping to explain any more.

Bettina Rand had obviously asked to do this interview. She was already sitting on one of the leather armchairs on the set, and she patted the other one invitingly, just as she had done for Kate. The look she gave Barry, though, was one that she reserved for males. 'Come on, big boy,' she said, her voice at its huskiest. 'It's nice to be playing opposite a hero type again. The last one was John Wayne himself. And my, you've got exactly his walk.'

Barry had always been good at imitations, and this seemed the right moment to try one. 'Sure have, ma'am,' he said, in an equally good impression of John Wayne's voice. In startling contrast to the shuddering Kate and the tense, stupid-looking Peter, he stalked on to the set as if he owned the studio and maybe the whole of Britannia TV. Somewhere deep inside, he was as nervous as they had been. But painful experience had taught him never to let fear show.

He reached his armchair just in time. A split second later, the lights brightened, a camera moved in and the recording began. Bettina started reading from her autocue.

'And now we have a really exciting, new-to-television test. Here by my side is Barry Bigley, the Dean Street Detective who specialises in getting the group out of trouble, even when they're in it up to their necks. On at least half-a-dozen occasions, I have been told, Barry has faced and beaten criminals with loaded guns – an astonishing record for someone who is still not quite thirteen. And I've also been told that he never blinked an eyelid. Is that right, Barry?'

Barry raised an eyebrow as coolly as Spock in *Star Trek*. 'I wouldn't say I was quite such a blinking – er, unblinking – marvel as all that,' he murmured.

Bettina's pleading eyes became warm and admiring. 'Well,' she told him, 'we'll all have a chance to see for ourselves what you do when you're faced with a gun. Because in a moment, an armed villain is going to come in here and tell us to reach for the skies.'

Barry raised both eyebrows this time. 'Reach for the skies? If I were Britannia TV, I'd get a less corny scriptwriter for a start,' he said, dusting an imaginary speck off his trousers.

That shook Bettina slightly. In fact, she blinked both eyelids. But she recovered herself rapidly, and managed a low, husky laugh.

'Anyway,' she went on, 'when he says that, I shall reach for them, like a good little helpless heroine. But what *you* do, Barry, is entirely up to you. The rules are simple. You have to pretend he's a real villain, with a real gun, firing real bullets instead of blanks. And you have fifteen seconds to get yourself – and me – out of his clutches. No holds barred, but if the gun goes off when it's pointed at a vital part of you, you'll have lost because officially you'll be dead. Do you understand?'

'Not quite,' said Barry. 'Suppose this turns into a roughhouse, and I accidentally hurt the actor? Is the poor man getting danger money?'

Bettina laughed. 'Big as you are for your age, I shouldn't worry too much about that. The actor we've chosen will be able to take care of himself, I promise you. Stand by. I think he's coming.'

The door on the set, the one leading to a mock-up of the dusty Dean Street basement corridor, full of rubber spiders and plastic cobwebs, burst open, and a masked actor came in, awkwardly brandishing a gun. He opened his mouth to say 'Reach for the skies', but remembered that this line had been criticised as corny. 'Er – er, stick 'em up, the pair of you!' he said instead, with a faint Irish accent. And he pointed the gun about midway between Barry and Bettina.

Bettina raised her hands, and for good measure, managed a loud scream. That couldn't have been in the script, thought Barry. The masked man started violently, and the nozzle of the gun wavered all over the place.

'This,' Barry told himself, 'is going to be a piece of cake . . .'

He rose up from the armchair and raised both hands above his head, as lazily as though he was having a good yawn and stretch. His fingers brushed against a poster – a copy of the one featuring Humphrey Bogart – which was on the wall behind him.

'Don't move a muscle, mister!' said the actor, struggling hard to sound ferocious. 'One move and you're – *aaah*!'

Barry had just ripped the poster off the wall and neatly wrapped it round his head. Taken completely aback, the man staggered blindly round the set, and it was child's play for Barry to snatch the gun out of his hand.

'End of test, I think,' he murmured to Bettina. 'Is it okay to take a bow?'

It was the actor who replied. 'Sure you can, laddie,' he said, obviously very angry. 'If you can take one – lying down!'

Barry was not as observant as Peter. He was only just beginning to realise that this actor was no ordinary man. Now that he looked hard at him, he could see enormous rippling muscles on his arms. 'Good grief!' he thought. 'They've hired a wrestler . . .'

A lot happened during the next split second. The man shook off the poster, and seizing Barry in what seemed like a karate hold, threw him halfway across the set, so that he landed, face downwards and completely winded, on the stretch of carpet in front of the door.

Before he could even begin to recover, the man had landed on top of him, and was not only pinning him down, but twisting his arm behind his back so painfully that it was all he could do not to scream for mercy. Through the pain, he could hear Bettina's voice – soft and husky again now, and very regretful.

'I'm afraid *this* Dean Street Detective is not going to pass,' she was announcing. 'He had fifteen seconds to beat the masked villain – and it's the eleventh second now. Twelve – thirteen – '

Still breathless, and in so much agony that he could hardly think, Barry was just about to grunt 'Okay, you win' when he suddenly realised something. It was his left arm that the masked wrestler was twisting so painfully. His right arm was still somewhere underneath him. And it was *still holding the gun*!

With a great effort, he managed to wrench it free; to point it at the masked villain, over his shoulder, and to fire – just as Bettina was counting 'Fifteen'.

There was only a blank in the gun, of course: a super-safe blank, to judge from the feeble 'pop' it made. But it was quite enough to put a blank expression on the villain's face. An expression that became even blanker as Barry murmured to Bettina: 'Would you mind asking this gentleman to let go of my arm and step off my back? After all, according to the rules you gave me, he *is* officially dead . . .'

8

The Big One

That, pretty obviously, really was the end of Barry's test.

Bettina Rand murmured hurried congratulations, and smiled at the camera as she finished: 'And so, like all good heroes, Barry Bigley has won through, ladies and gentlemen, and rescued this very grateful heroine . . . '

The cameras stopped whirring; the lights dimmed slightly, and the man in the mask at last released Barry's arm and stood up. More than that, he took off his mask, and introduced himself as Paddy Reilly, amateur wrestler and professional special effects man and stunt arranger. 'I've got the job of staging all the tricks and tests on the show,' he said. "Tis sorry I am I lost my temper, laddie, but it's not easy to take being made a fool of by a twelve-year-old. No hard feelings, I'm hoping.'

He held out his hand.

Barry took it reluctantly. His left arm was still stiff and aching, and he didn't want the same treatment to be meted out to the right one. But he needn't have worried. Reilly's grip this time was as warm and friendly as his sunny Irish smile.

'Sure and it's delighted I am to be meeting a member of such a brilliant team,' he said. 'You and your friends have made mincemeat of the producer and me all morning. The score so far, by my reckoning, must be Dean Street Detectives 100 and the rest of us nothin' but nil.'

Barry frowned. 'But you people aren't fighting us – you're

testing us,' he said. 'Surely it makes a better television programme if we come through?'

An odd, warning expression crossed Paddy Reilly's face – and his voice dropped to a whisper. 'Some folks don't like kids showing them where they get off,' he said, 'and Mr Philip Beatty is one of them. I'd be very careful from now on, if I were –'

He broke off, as the door of the control room crashed open, and Beatty himself came striding back on to the scene, his face crimson, his black beard jutting forward as menacingly as a fist about to strike. 'Right!' he shouted. 'Now we come to the crunch. The final test – and the toughest of them all! It's taking place in another part of the studio. And I want all four Dean Street Detectives to come along with me. And you, Bettina. And you, Paddy. And David Reynolds . . .'

'Everybody onstage for the finale, it sounds like,' murmured Barry, as Anne, Peter and Kate came up to him, and they all found themselves following the bearded producer. Bettina and Paddy were behind them. David Reynolds and Rosalie Penrose, who had unexpectedly joined the party, brought up the rear.

'There's something unfair about all this,' said Kate. 'Barry, Peter and I have all had solo tests. Why doesn't Anne get one?'

Philip Beatty overheard her. Over his shoulder, he barked: 'There's a simple answer to that. Anne is supposed to be your leader, isn't she? Well, how can you test a leader unless she's got somebody to lead?'

'You mean,' said Anne, 'you're going to test me on how well I give orders to the others?'

'But that's screwy,' said Kate. 'Anne doesn't give us orders, not when we're in action. She just says "Let's go" and we – er, each do our own thing.' She frowned. That didn't sound quite right – and it certainly didn't explain the Dean Street Detectives' extraordinary knack of suddenly behaving like a well-drilled team in an emergency. 'Er, that is, we each do our own thing *together*,' she finished.

Somewhere behind them, Paddy Reilly laughed. 'That makes perfect sense to me, being as Irish as you are, Katie Murphy, but I doubt if the others will be following you at all.'

'All I can say is,' snarled Beatty, 'that if in this test, Anne doesn't give any orders, or the rest don't carry out the ones she does give, then she's going to score nought out of ten as a leader, and you're going to score nought out of ten as a team!'

The idea of that seemed to please him immensely. He was chuckling somewhere deep in his beard as he led them up a flight of metal steps and along a narrow gangway, with wire mesh on either side. They were at quite a height, not far below the studio ceiling.

'Well, that's the set we've built for you down there,' said Beatty, almost proudly. 'As you can see, it's going to be quite a test.'

The Dean Street Detectives gasped.

They were looking down on what appeared to be a complicated mass of sloping roofs, dominated by a tall chimney stack. Obviously the design had been based on the roof which they had shown Miss Penrose and her photographer a couple of days before. But the tiles had been made to slope so steeply that to cross them would be like tackling a Commando assault course.

'I thought,' said Katie, 'this was just going to be a scene from one of our adventures. You were going to show how we escaped across the roofs from that Mafia gang.'

'Yes, that was the original idea, dear,' Miss Penrose said. 'But Mr Beatty thought that it would make it more fun to alter the roofs, and turn the whole thing into a challenge.'

'A very exciting challenge at that,' said Paddy. 'I'm going to put on my mask again, and me and one or two friends are going to pretend to be the Mafia gang. The idea is, we come

54

after you with guns blazing, and it'll be Anne's job to get you across the tiles and up to that chimney before we can catch up with you. That's right, isn't it, Mr Beatty?'

'Perfectly correct,' Beatty said. 'And so the scene will be at one and the same time a leadership test for Anne, a re-staging of a real-life Dean Street Detectives adventure, an exciting exercise in its own right *and* a spectacular finish for the first half of the programme. Okay?'

For once, he didn't sound as though he was sneering. It was almost as if he was carried away by the sheer orginality of the whole idea.

'When all's said and done, you've got to hand it to Mr Beatty,' Paddy Reilly murmured. 'He may be tough to work with and hard on kids, but there's a touch of sheer genius there somewhere.'

The Dean Street Detectives weren't so sure. Peter's eyes narrowed as he stared at those roofs below them – at the steep gulleys between them, and steeply sloping angles of the tiles. He wondered what they were really made of. Thin hardboard, he imagined, that might give at any time. Scrambling across them under pressure, obeying orders from a bellowing sister, wasn't his idea of fun at all.

Kate was looking equally doubtful. 'That chimney stack,' she said, 'looks as if it's going to topple over before we even start.'

'Oh, no it won't,' laughed Paddy Reilly. 'It's a bit special, that stack. The only thing on the set that's really made of brick. And we've concreted it into the floor. There's a commentator's box concealed behind it, where Mr Reynolds is going to sit and describe the whole exercise. Aren't you, Mr Reynolds?'

David Reynolds grunted something they couldn't catch. Peter glanced round at him. Reynolds was looking as nervous as ever, his forehead glistening with sweat above those large square spectacles. Was he right? *Was* there someone out to get him – and danger for him everywhere on this show? The sight of him made Peter uneasier than ever.

Anne was secretly feeling very uneasy, too. As she had so often said, as long as she was their leader, the Dean Street Detectives didn't turn away from challenges. And she was proud to think that her test was going to be the big one – the toughest test for herself and for them all.

But supposing she blew it? Supposing she hesitated, and gave confused orders – with all those cameras turning, all those millions going to watch –

Barry saw her doubtful expression, and whispered: 'Come on, fearless leader. You've really *got* to be fearless now.'

Nobody ever made an appeal like that to Anne in vain. She straightened her shoulders, pushed past Barry, and was suddenly striding confidently along immediately behind Philip Beatty . . . leading the Dean Street Detectives into one of the strangest – and, as it turned out, most terrifying episodes of their entire career.

9

Exercise Rooftop

It took Philip Beatty a long time to get everybody in position, and everything ready, for what he called 'Exercise Rooftop'. It was one of the most complicated scenes that had ever been staged in Studio One.

The expanse of roofs occupied the greater part of the studio floor – a space as big as a couple of tennis courts laid side by side. The designer had followed the photographs of the original roof quite closely in one respect: in the middle of the set was a skylight, just like the one the Dean Street Detectives had shown to Rosalie Penrose. Surrounding it was a small ledge, a few metres square, which was the only flat surface on the set. Once away from that, there were tiles sloping away at terrifying angles, shaky-looking gables, flimsy bits of guttering – in fact, a fearful course to scramble over, towered over by the one rock-solid (or rather, brick-solid) object in sight: the massive chimney stack from behind which David Reynolds was to do his commentary.

The scene was to begin with the Dean Street Detectives coming up through the skylight. Then, when they were poised on the surrounding ledge, there were to be revolver shots from below, followed by the crash of breaking glass and Paddy Reilly and his friends were to come bursting through the skylight, in full pursuit. That was to be the signal for the big roof chase, during which Anne had to get herself, Barry, Peter and Kate over the tiles and up to the chimney before Paddy & Co could catch them. Before the Dean Street

Detectives emerged through the skylight, Bettina Rand was to stand on the ledge, telling the audience what was going to happen. When the action began, she was to hand over to David Reynolds, who was not only to do the commentary on the scene, but was also to be the judge. Being behind the chimney, he was obviously right at the winning-post.

That was the basic Beatty plan – but he had forgotten one thing: since the roofs were really resting on the studio floor, the skylight didn't actually lead anywhere. There was nothing below it except solid wood, which meant that while Bettina was doing her introduction bit, the Dean Street Detectives and Paddy & Co – four fairly large children and four very large adults – would be crammed together in a space no bigger than the average garden frame!

Another producer would have changed his plan, or waited until the set was rearranged. But not Philip Beatty. 'It's only for two or three minutes,' he said. 'Shouldn't hurt anyone being cooped up for a little time like that.'

It did not turn out to be for two or three minutes. First, Bettina's autocue went wrong; then a spotlight fused; then a cameraman started arguing about the angle he was expected to zoom in from. By the time all this had been sorted out, more than a quarter of an hour had gone by – and the Dean Street Detectives were half-paralysed with cramp.

'This is awful,' said Kate. 'How can he possibly expect us to jump up and go careering across sloping tiles after this? What's he trying to do – kill us all?'

'That's quite possible,' said Peter softly. 'There's something strange going on in this studio. Something we haven't even begun to grasp.'

'Well, all I know,' murmured Barry, 'is that something strange is going on in my left ear, and I rather think it's Kate's toe arriving. If you'd mind moving it just a fraction, Katie me darling –'

58

'Move it?' said Kate shakily. 'I can't even feel it. That whole leg went numb five minutes ago.'

'This is ridiculous,' announced Anne. 'And I don't see why we should put up with it. The moment we're allowed out, I'm going to make a formal protest. Then they'll have to stop the recording and give us a chance to recover.'

For a moment, they had forgotten that they had company. Paddy Reilly and his friends were all somewhere in this human sardine-can too.

'Mr Beatty's not a man to stop a recording once it's started,' Paddy warned them. 'He's more likely to call off the test and claim that you four threw in the towel. But don't worry. It won't be much of a chase. Your masked pursuers are just as paralysed as you are!'

Bettina Rand had finished her introduction at last. Anne could see a camera hovering like a low-flying helicopter just above the skylight, and the cameraman was signalling her to move.

She opened the skylight with a bang, and found herself staggering out on to the flat bit of roof, followed by Peter, Barry and Kate, all of them moving as stiffly as robots – and rusty, creaking robots at that.

Anne blinked round her. It was impossible to see anything beyond the circle of brilliant light in which they were bathed. Every arc lamp on the ceiling, and every other spotlight in the studio, seemed to be trained on them, so that they were not only half-paralysed, but half-blinded too. She was about to ignore Paddy's warning, and go ahead with her protest. But at that moment, she heard Bettina's voice. The ex-film star had stepped out of the spotlight, but was evidently still being heard on sound.

'Ah! Now here come the Dean Street Detectives!' she was saying brightly. 'They've spent the last quarter of an hour terribly cooped up, but as you can see, they're as ready for action as ever . . .'

'The only action I'm ready for,' said Kate to herself, 'is a backward flip into a dead faint.' She didn't feel like saying anything aloud, though, with all those mikes and cameras zooming in on their every word and every movement . . .

'And now,' continued Bettina briskly, 'I'm handing you over to Mr *TV Investigates* himself, David Reynolds, to give you a moment-by-moment commentary as Anne Miller and her gallant team re-enact one of their greatest adventures – and take up the challenge of the final test. Take it away, David . . .'

They couldn't hear how David Reynolds 'took it away'. His commentary box was supposed to be soundproof. But they could hear the sound of his voice barking and braying as excitedly as though he was describing a boxing championship fight.

What he was saying, Anne couldn't imagine. After all, they weren't doing anything. Peter, Kate and Barry were all just standing dazedly, waiting – for – for –

Her orders, she suddenly realised, with a violent start. They couldn't move without them.

She struggled to think of a command, but her brain seemed as paralysed as her limbs. Just then, the roar of a revolver shot and the crash of breaking glass came from the direction of the skylight. Nothing had been fired and nothing broken, a sound-effects loudspeaker had taken care of it all, but this, she remembered, was their cue.

As the skylight opened again, and the masked figure of Paddy Reilly came bounding out, she gave her first command. It was the obvious one, but she couldn't help that: at least it would get things moving.

'Right!' she heard herself saying, as if from a long way away. 'L-l-let's go!'

In a real-life adventure, that would have been enough to send the Dean Street Detectives careering down the sloping tiles in the direction of the chimney. After all, they all knew where they had to head. But that wouldn't have won her any marks for leadership, as both Peter and Barry realised. They both stayed rooted to the spot.

'Which of us go where?' whispered Barry softly.

'Don't you realise, dear sister?' added Peter, in an equally low whisper. 'You have to *say*.'

Anne hurriedly pointed down the tiles, and barked: 'You first, Barry. Then you, Peter. Then Kate –'

She broke off. Kate, awkward as ever, hadn't been waiting for orders like the others. She had been screwing up her courage, and now, suddenly, she hurled herself off the ledge ahead of the rest. Her cramped limbs couldn't cope with the steep slope. She fell forward, and the next moment, was half-rolling, half-slithering helplessly down towards a bit of fake guttering at the bottom.

She landed with a fearful bump, and a scream that threatened to shatter every microphone on the set.

Great! thought Anne in a near panic. First she'd failed to give clear orders. Then her orders had been clearly disobeyed. Somehow, she couldn't exactly see her marks piling up . . .

Barry and Peter *had* obeyed her by this time. They were both clattering and scrambling down the slope to Kate's side. Barry somehow managed it smoothly and effortlessly. Peter, as usual, bungled it completely, rolled and slithered as helplessly as Kate, and finished up landing head first right on top of her. Kate screamed again, more piercingly than ever.

'Gerrof me, Peter. Oh, ouch! – I've twisted something – my ankle, I think –'

This obviously called for fresh orders, and Anne promptly started to give them. 'If Kate's really hurt, we'll have to carry her. Barry, take her arms. Peter, grab her legs –'

61

She broke off, and whirled round just in time to see Paddy Reilly creeping up behind her. He was moving stiffly and clumsily, his arms stretched out in front of him, like a zombie in a late-night horror movie – but he had nearly reached her, and as she turned, his fingers were almost brushing her face. If he touched her, it would count as capture by the enemy, and her test would be over!

Shaken and startled, Anne ducked and backed away – clean over the edge of the flat stretch of roof. Before she knew it, she was sliding down it, head over heels, banging into everything and dislodging tiles for all the world like a human avalanche.

Down below, Barry and Peter had just succeeded in picking up Kate, who was struggling and screaming 'I'm all right, I tell you. I can manage. Leave me alone! Leave me –'

That was when Anne arrived, knocking all of them clean off their feet, so that the whole team became a helpless tangle of flailing arms and legs. They picked themselves up; sorted themselves out; thought of the mikes and cameras trained on them and the millions who would be watching – and then did something that took Philip Beatty and everyone else at Britannia TV completely by surprise.

They all four of them burst out laughing.

'And now, ladies and gentlemen,' said Barry, squinting up at an overhead camera that seemed to be moving in for a close shot, 'for our next total disaster –'

Anne had stopped seeing the funny side of things by that time. She knew she had obviously scored nought out of ten, and had created a cosmically comic shambles. But giving up was not in her nature, and the test wasn't quite over yet.

Suddenly she was, at last, very much the leader of the team.

'Stop messing about, all of you!' she barked. 'We've only got seconds now to get up to that chimney. But we *can* do it. Follow me!'

Putting an arm round Kate, who was still only able to hobble, she led the way along a narrow ridge, over three high, awkward gables, and even managed to encourage Kate across a difficult jump. Barry and Peter kept right behind her, Barry relaxed and chuckling, Peter grunting and groaning. Paddy and the masked pursuers must be somewhere behind her, she knew, but they had fallen so far back that they weren't in sight.

They were now on what was really the homestretch – the final challenge of the test: about ten metres of steeply sloping tiles which led straight up to the chimney stack. The slope was very steep indeed.

'We'll never make it up there if we take it slowly,' said Anne, thinking aloud. 'We'll have to run at it, and try to reach the top in one dash. Linking arms, I think, so that if anyone falls back, he – or she – will be carried forward with the rest.'

'Supposing we all fall back?' asked Kate. It was the sort of remark she would make.

'Then we take another run-up and try again,' said Anne, not very patiently. 'And as for your ankle – if we're quick, it needn't even touch the ground!'

It was a pretty crazy, reckless scheme – entirely typical of Anne. But strangely enough, they all had a feeling it could work.

Looking exactly as though they were about to sing Auld Lang Syne, the Dean Street Detectives drew back from the slope, and linked arms. They paused for a moment to take a deep breath – and Peter's sharp ears could just hear the excited voice of David Reynolds yelling into a microphone in the commentary box on the other side of the stack. He obviously fancied himself as a sports commentator.

'Oh, what a come-back this has been for the Dean Streeters! After that shambolic start, they've pulled themselves together and tackled the course like Olympic athletes.

They've even taken Kate's unfortunate ankle injury literally in their stride. And now, as they come up to that daunting sprint up the finishing slope, they look as relaxed and confident as –'

Peter couldn't hear any more. Anne shouted 'Ready. Steady. Go!' and they were off, hurdling through a six-metre run-up and then hurling themselves at the tiles. With Barry striding, Peter staggering, Kate hopping and Anne crashing forward in her usual avalanche style, they made an extraordinary team, but somehow a miraculously successful one. They had linked arms so determinedly that they cancelled out each other's weaknesses. Peter slowed Barry down, but Barry speeded up Peter. Having to half-carry the hopping Kate made Anne go more carefully, but doubled her determination. About two-thirds of the way up the slope, it did seem as though they'd lost their impetus, and could do nothing but slide and slither back and down. But Anne and Barry, both sweating and grunting as though they were taking part in a tug of war, closed their eyes and struggled on – and suddenly they'd made it!

There were the bricks of the chimney stack right in front of them – and there was Barry reaching out to get a grip on them with his one free hand . . .

A split second later, they were all four of them off the slope, and on a tiny, metre-length ledge of concrete at the base of the chimney-stack, leaning back against the bricks and gasping.

From the other side, they could hear David Reynolds, his voice very loud and clear now, shouting: 'And here they are, all four of them, at the chimney, well ahead of their pursuers! And as official judge of this test, I'm happy to declare that –'

That was when it happened – the thing that the Dean Street Detectives would remember with a shudder for the rest of their lives. Without the slightest warning, and, it appeared, without the slightest reason, the solid brick chimney stack, 'concreted into the floor', according to Paddy Reilly, *started to sway away from them.*

'My God!' said Barry. 'What the –'

His voice was hoarse – and Peter's was hoarser as he yelled, sharply, wildly: 'David! David, can you hear me? *Watch out –*'

The chimney wasn't just swaying now. It was breaking up and falling – right on top of the little glass commentary box immediately behind it.

David Reynolds obviously hadn't heard Peter's shout, hadn't heard anything.

'– I'm happy to declare that the Dean Street Detectives have passed *triumphantly* –' he was yelling into his mike.

He never finished the sentence. His voice was drowned by the thunderous, earthquake-like roar as the chimney came crashing down. The whole floor of the studio shook. Bricks cascaded everywhere, momentarily filling the air with a thick white fog of plaster dust. When it cleared, the little glass box had totally disappeared beneath a pile of bricks and rubble.

And no sound was coming from it – nothing but the most terrible silence the Dean Street Detectives had ever known.

10

The Ideal Adventure

Studio One didn't stay silent for long. Within a second, bells were ringing, sirens wailing, people rushing everywhere.

Barry moved first and fastest. He had scrambled down to the pile of rubble, and was frantically struggling to pull away bricks, even before the first siren sounded. Anne scrambled down to join him, with Peter and Kate right behind her. None of them spoke. They were all too terrified at the thought of what they might find . . .

Paddy Reilly and his friends, all looking grotesquely out of place in their masks, joined them. Paddy's eyes were staring through his mask with blank disbelief. 'Rock solid, the chimney was, the one rock-solid thing on the set –'

Other helpers were appearing now. A great crowd of them: technicians, camera crew members, and finally ambulance-men and a policeman. The policeman ordered everyone except the ambulance-men off the set.

'Rescue work like this is best left to experts,' he said. 'The rest of you could do more harm than good.' He looked at the Dean Street Detectives, whose faces were covered with dust, and whose hands were red and bloody from their frantic struggle with the bricks. 'Though bless you for trying, kids,' he said. 'If anyone's done their best for whoever's under there, *you* have.'

'It was the least they could do,' said a harsh, sneering voice, 'seeing that they knocked the ruddy chimney over in the first place.'

The Detectives didn't need to look round to realise that Philip Beatty was back on the scene.

When, about ten minutes later, the ambulance-men finally reached him, David Reynolds was found to be alive and all in one piece, although unconscious. Clearly, he needed to be rushed to hospital.

A hush fell over the studio while he was being carried out on a stretcher. Then everyone began talking at once.

'They're terrifying, these accidents on the set,' came the husky voice of Bettina Rand. 'I remember when Marilyn Monroe and I were –'

Rosalie Penrose obviously didn't want to hear about that. 'That *poor* Mr Reynolds!' she was saying. 'And he threw his whole heart and soul into the programme! I was listening to his commentary in the control room, and honestly, you'd think the children were Torvill and Dean and Sebastian Coe rolled into one.'

Philip Beatty grunted with disgust. 'If we're not careful, this whole programme is going to sound like a broadcast by the Dean Street Detectives Fan Club!' he snorted.

He turned to glare at Anne, Peter, Kate and Barry. 'You haven't heard what you're in for next, have you?' he snarled at them. 'Then you've got quite a shock coming. Miss Penrose here had the bright idea of asking the children in ten selected schools in the Britannia TV area to make up an ideal adventure for the Dean Street Detectives.'

'An ideal adventure?' stammered Peter.

'F–for *us*?' shouted Kate.

'How very kind of them,' drawled Barry.

'We're – er – highly honoured,' said Anne.

Philip Beatty flashed them that white, shark-like smile.

'You won't feel so pleased when you start filming the winning adventure tomorrow morning,' he said. 'We're going to use it as the final climax to the show. It was made up by an eight-year-old called Emma Jane Morrison, and you can take my word for it – it's got everything! It features you escaping down a rope-ladder from a helicopter, landing on the roof of an express train, and having a running fight there with a masked arch-villain.'

There was a long, startled pause. Then: 'We're doing all that – tomorrow?' said Kate faintly.

'That's right,' Beatty said. 'So make sure you're not late.'

His smile became even more shark-like as he added: 'And let's hope – for your sakes – that there are no more accidents . . .'

He sounded as though he was still blaming them for the last one. Or trying to turn suspicion on to them, Peter thought . . .

All through the drive back to Fenton, Peter sat silent, remembering the things David Reynolds had said to him. '*I'm in a spot . . . I've been investigating someone who's very dangerous indeed . . . There have been so many attempts on my life I'm scared – very scared, as you can see . . .*' And, Peter recollected, when he had asked Reynolds if that someone was connected with the programme, he had nodded before changing his mind, and turning the nod into a shrug. The more he thought about it, the surer he became that that falling chimney hadn't been an accident – but the latest of the attempts to kill David Reynolds by that dangerous someone on the show.

Anne, Kate and Barry were thinking along exactly the same lines.

'That sheet of paper you snatched from David Reynolds's clipboard,' said Anne. 'Have you still got it?'

'Of course I have, dear sister,' snapped Peter. 'And I can't wait to get home and start treating it.'

Suddenly neither could the others. When the car arrived outside the Millers' home, all four Dean Street Detectives shot past a startled Mrs Miller, hardly saying a word, and didn't stop until they reached Peter's bedroom, where he kept a spare magnifying glass and a box of fingerprint powder.

He spread out the sheet, and dusted it with the powder, which not only brought up fingerprints, but made every scratch and dent in the paper show. Then he, and the others, groaned with disappointment. All that remained of the dangerous name that had been written on the top sheet were two capital letters with a faint line between them, like this:

$$P \longrightarrow P$$

'Well, that doesn't get us very far,' said Kate. 'There's no one in the case, as far as we know, with the initials "PP".'

'They may not both be Ps,' Peter told her. 'For instance, if you write a B or an R and don't press hard enough on the finishing stroke, *they* could come out on the sheet underneath looking like Ps.'

Anne tensed. 'If that second P is really a B,' she said, 'then the name could be Philip Beatty.'

'But then,' Barry pointed out, 'if the second P is really an R, it could be Paddy Reilly.'

'And if the first P is an R,' said Kate, 'it could be Rosalie Penrose. And if the first P is a B, and the second one an R, you could even just get Bettina Rand.'

'Full house!' said Barry wryly. 'In other words, we're right back where we started. It could have been just about anybody we've met at the studios.'

Peter frowned. He had a feeling that there was a clue he'd missed, staring him right in the face – but he had been peering so hard at the sheet that the letters, even under the magnifying glass, were now swimming in front of his eyes.

'You're probably right,' he said, very reluctantly. 'I just hope –'

He stopped, his eyes narrowing.

'You just hope what?' said Kate crossly. She had forgotten

about her ankle, which had turned out to be only slightly twisted, but she had suddenly stepped on it and got a painful twinge.

'I just hope,' said Peter slowly, 'that the owner of this name doesn't think that David Reynolds told me what it was. If so, with his or her talent for staging accidents –'

Barry finished the sentence for him, in his usual mocking style. 'We could,' he murmured, 'be in for a far from ideal adventure.'

11

The Falling Crate

That night, Anne, Peter and Kate reached a big decision. They decided to tell Mr and Mrs Miller almost everything about what had happened that day – including David Reynolds's talk of a dangerous enemy on the set.

'It's only right that Dad should be brought into this,' Anne had said. 'For all we know, the enemy might try to get at David Reynolds in hospital – maybe while he's still unconscious! He ought to have police protection.'

Peter nodded. 'Dad won't be able to arrange that, of course – it's way out of his area. But he can make a phone call to the head of the Kettlewell CID.'

'Are you going to tell him about the eavesdropper outside the door while David was talking to Peter?' said Kate. 'If he knows about that, he might reckon that *we* need police protection, too.'

'He's more likely to stop us appearing on the show altogether,' said Peter. 'And I wouldn't be sorry if he did.'

The idea of climbing down a rope-ladder from a helicopter was already beginning to give him the shivers. To say nothing of jumping from it on to the roof of a train –

Anne sniffed scornfully. She never had the slightest sympathy with her brother's nerves. 'We've signed a contract,' she pointed out. '*And* we've recorded half the programme. It just wouldn't be fair to anyone to back out now. They're all depending on us.'

Kate nodded gravely. She was secretly getting as scared as Peter, but at the same time, she was feeling as proud as Anne. And the feeling of pride won. 'It's a great responsibility,' she said, 'being the stars of a show.'

'Right,' said Anne. 'Then we tell Dad and Mum everything – except about the eavesdropper. Okay?'

Things were very far from okay with Detective Superintendent Miller when he had listened to their stories. He turned crimson with fury.

'You should have told me all this about David Reynolds at once! Attempts may have been made on his life at that hospital already. The ambulance could even have been waylaid . . .' He rushed to the phone, dialled Directory Inquiries, and asked for the number of Kettlewell Police Station. While he was waiting for it, he continued to lecture them over his shoulder. 'Apart from that, it's too late by now to stop the bricks and rubble being cleared away from Studio One. What chance will the police there have of finding evidence of attempted murder?'

Directory Inquiries got him the number, and in a minute he was having a long conversation with the Kettlewell police inspector.

'He's checking with the hospital, and sending a man there right away,' he told them, as he hung up the receiver. 'Let's hope and pray it's in time.'

To the children's surprise, he dialled Directory Inquiries again, and asked for the number of the Britannia TV studios.

'I'm ringing this Philip Beatty,' he told them, 'to inform him that unless he changes his plans for tomorrow, I am forbidding you to take any further part in *Twenty-First Century People*. What he's proposing is absolutely outrageous. Children leaping in and out of helicopters, fighting villains on train-roofs, it all sounds extremely dangerous and totally illegal. And if he dares to mention that contract you've signed, I suggest that the three of you cover your ears up.

Because I'm going to tell him precisely what he can do with *that*!'

Philip Beatty was apparently working late at the studio. At all events, when Mr Miller obtained – and rang – the Britannia number, the producer came on the telephone straight away. He was probably sorry that he did. Mr Miller yelled at him for a full three minutes without pausing for breath, ending by roaring: 'So what are you trying to do to these children – kill the lot of them? Because that's what it sounds like to me.'

Philip Beatty was not a good person to roar at. He simply roared back, his loud, sneering tones so piercing that Anne, Peter and Kate could hear every word he said, as clearly as Mr Miller himself. 'In that case, Superintendent, it is obvious that you know nothing about the television business,' he thundered. 'I can assure you that there will be absolutely no risk to the children at all. Let me spell out for you exactly what we're proposing to do.'

He sounded so patronising that he might have been talking to a six year old.

'I'd be much obliged if you would,' Mr Miller said heavily.

'First of all then,' Beatty went on, 'let's take the helicopter scene. Oh, yes, they'll have to go up in a helicopter, and climb down a ladder from it – but the machine will actually be flying only about six metres up, above a swimming pool. The bottom of the ladder will be barely two metres above the water, and even if they fall, they'll only get a soaking.'

Mr Miller still sounded doubtful. 'In that case, how are you going to film them jumping from the rope-ladder on to the roof of a train?'

Beatty took a deep breath. He now sounded as though he was talking to a *two* year old. 'The train shot will be filmed an hour later, in a different location. As a matter of fact, we'll be using Kettlewell Amateur Steam Railway. I thought it would be a novelty to have the Dean Street Detectives jumping on to the roof of an old fashioned steam train. But they won't be doing it from a helicopter. In fact, there will be no choppers in this scene at all. The children will be seen climbing down a rope-ladder, but it will be fixed to a railway bridge which the camera won't show. And they won't actually have to do anything but hang there while the train passes below.'

'What roof *will* they jump down on, then?' Mr Miller demanded.

'A fake train roof we're rigging up in the studio. That's where they'll do their fighting with the villain, and so on. We'll have a special effects machine to rock it realistically from side to side.'

His father was now looking so totally bewildered that Peter thought he'd take a hand.

'Don't you see, Dad? We're going to film three separate scenes. One climbing out of a helicopter on to a dangling rope-ladder. One dangling from a rope-ladder above a roaring steam train. And one jumping on to a fake train roof, and fighting a villain on it. When they're shown quickly one after the other, it'll look as though we're taking incredible risks –'

'But in fact,' finished Anne, 'there'll be no risks at all. The chopper will only be flying a few metres above a swimming-pool; we'll never set foot on the train – we'll just see it go roaring past beneath us; and the train roof will be just a platform in the studio, with a machine rocking it from side to side.'

Philip Beatty evidently heard all that at his end of the phone. He started laughing, in his thick, sneering way.

'Your children seem to have grasped the situation, Superintendent, even if you haven't,' he said. 'Are you satisfied now that I'm not going to kill them after all?'

Mr Miller gave a grunt, which Beatty took to mean 'yes'.

'Right, then,' he said. 'Our car will be along to pick the kids up tomorrow at half past six, and I'll look forward to seeing them at the studios at nine. I hope they get a good night's sleep. Tomorrow should be a big day for them. If you'll excuse me now, Mr Miller, I have a lot of work –'

'Just a minute,' Mr Miller suddenly roared. 'You can cancel that studio car!' There was a second of glum silence, while the Detectives' hopes of being dashing film stars shrank to a total zero. Then he went on: 'I've just decided to take the day off and bring them up myself. Your studio seems a little accident-prone, Mr Beatty. Perhaps it won't be, with a CID man looking on.'

Beatty sounded taken aback. It was as though the last thing he wanted was the Superintendent hanging around the studio all day. 'You'll be – er – very welcome, of course, Mr Miller,' he said, very unconvincingly. 'And bring Mrs Miller too, if you wish. But I do assure you – there is absolutely no risk . . .'

He was still insisting there was 'absolutely no risk' the following morning, when he led Detective Superintendent and Mrs Miller, with Anne, Peter, Kate and Barry just behind them, across a yard at the back of the studio towards a waiting Outside Broadcast van.

The Detective Superintendent eyed the van dubiously. 'And just where is this going to take us?' he demanded.

'To Kettlewell heliport,' Philip Beatty told him. 'We're starting with the helicopter scene. But, as I told you, it will be flying low over a swimming pool, and there will be –'

The Dean Street Detectives said it for him this time. All four of them chorused: 'Absolutely no risk at –'

The sentence was never finished – or, rather, it ended in frantic screams and shrieks. The studio yard was a big place, and a lot of unloading was going on. Peter had suddenly noticed that a heavy crate, being swung by a small crane right above their heads, looked as though it was coming off the hook. His heart suddenly pounding, he yelled: '*That crate – it's falling! Look OU –*'

The Dean Street Detectives had often moved fast during their hectic careers – but they had never moved faster than now. Peter leaped one way, Anne another, and Barry – dragging a screaming Kate – a third. Mrs Miller seemed rooted to the spot, staring up helplessly. Mr Miller seized her hand, and pulled her back so hastily that he didn't look where he was going. He collided with Philip Beatty, and fell sprawling.

In the micro-second before the crate fell, all the Dean Street Detectives realised that Mr Miller was lying in its path. But it had landed, with a rending, splintering, reverberating crash, before they could do anything about him at all.

12

On With The Show

For the second time in twenty-four hours, the Dean Street Detectives felt the ground shaking beneath them. The crate landed so close that the shock waves jarred their whole bodies. At the same instant, it burst open, and splintering wood flew everywhere, making it impossible to see Mr Miller.

Just as on the previous day, a fog of choking dust came up – but this time, when it cleared, there wasn't a terrible silence. Mr Miller's voice could be heard loud and clear, calling all of them by turn. 'Peter! Anne! Kate! Barry! Are you . . . all right?'

They rushed forward from all directions, picking their way through the dust and wood splinters, and found the Detective Superintendent lying on his back, with a shaken but unhurt Mrs Miller bending over him. He had one foot trapped beneath the wreckage.

'We're fine, Dad,' Anne told him. 'But – but what about you?'

Now that he was satisfied that the whole family was safe, Mr Miller suddenly realised his own plight. 'I'm afraid I'm very far from fine,' he grunted. 'Leg's broken, I think. In two places, I shouldn't wonder.'

The figure of Philip Beatty loomed out of the dust.

'Absolutely no risk, eh?' Mr Miller shouted at him. 'There'll be a full police inquiry into this, Beatty, I promise you. And if all of us, especially the kids, hadn't moved like lightning, you'd be facing charges of gross negligence – maybe manslaughter – maybe even *murder* –' He was suddenly roaring at the top of his voice. Oddly enough, that made Anne feel a lot happier. There couldn't be too much wrong with Dad if he could shout like that, she thought. When really bad – even with something like the flu – he hardly said a word.

Beatty made no reply to this onslaught. He simply waved to someone the other side of the yard. Almost at once, ambulance men appeared with a stretcher. The next second, the ambulance itself was arriving a few metres away. Everyone except Mrs Miller was made to stand back. Within minutes, the Detective Superintendent's foot had been freed, and he was on the stretcher, being carried towards the ambulance, with a dazed Mrs Miller hurrying alongside. The next thing Anne knew, both her parents had been whisked into the ambulance, and it was driving away.

'Honestly,' she said, 'they might have given Mum a chance to wave us goodbye.'

'Don't fuss, children,' Philip Beatty told them. 'The sooner Mr Miller is got to hospital, the better it'll be for that leg of his. I assure you, he'll be very well looked after – Kettlewell Hospital is one of the best in Britain. And of course he has Mrs Miller with him, so you've nothing to worry about at all.'

'No,' Anne felt like saying. 'But *you'll* have something to worry about – when Dad starts that police inquiry . . .'

In fact, she said nothing. Beatty didn't give her a chance. Scarcely pausing for breath, he folded his arms and went on: 'Now I daresay this has been rather a shock to you – Mr Miller is right, we *do* seem to be accident-prone here at the moment – but we've a tight schedule to meet, so please follow me.'

He led the way across to the Outside Broadcast van, and held the door open for them at the rear. Peter didn't like his expression. He could have been a huge spider welcoming four juicy flies into its larder. Anne didn't like it either, but didn't think they had much choice.

'We *are* under contract – and I suppose the show must go on,' she said, and strode off in the direction of the van, calling over her shoulder: 'We mustn't hang about, or they'll think we're scared.'

The other Dean Street Detectives followed reluctantly – and in Peter's case, very shakily. Even Barry couldn't quite manage his usual cool, casual stroll. 'I wish someone would tell our fearless leader,' he said, his voice starting gruff, but suddenly becoming high-pitched and squeaky, 'that sometimes scared is the *sensible* thing to be!'

Whether it was sensible or not, the Dean Street Detectives had plenty to be scared about all through the shooting of the helicopter scene.

It was the first time any of them had been on a helicopter trip. Normally they would have found it an exciting experience, but their secret fears made it terrifying. Supposing the person behind all these accidents had got at the aircraft? Supposing that whirling vane, just above them, had been tampered with, so that when they reached a certain speed, it would fly off and send them plummeting? Or supposing the other helicopter, the one flying alongside them with a television camera, got too close and –

Fortunately for their nerves, the trip was very short; almost short enough to go in the Guinness Book of Records, Barry thought. In less than twenty seconds, Paddy Reilly, their pilot, brought it down low to hover over the Kettlewell swimming pool. Philip Beatty, who was crouching at the back out of range of the camera, shouted: 'This is it. Get cracking, one of you. Open the door and start paying out the rope-ladder. It's just over there on the floor. And there's no need to be frightened. If you look down, you'll see we're only three or four metres off the ground – or rather, water . . .'

''Tis right enough, that,' said Paddy. 'Even if you take a tumble, 'twill be no worse than jumping into the deep end from a high diving board. *And* they've got ambulance-men down there in case anything goes wrong.'

'Ambulance-men,' said Kate, 'seem to be the busiest people at Britannia TV.'

It was rather a poor joke, and she wasn't surprised when nobody laughed. She didn't feel much like laughing herself. She was beginning to feel sick – though whether seasick or airsick it was hard to say. The hovering helicopter was shuddering so furiously that it was shaking every bone in their bodies. And it was making the water heave and slurp like a stormy sea. The other helicopter with the camera was still alongside, doubling the noise and the wind.

'Get cracking, I said!' barked Philip Beatty. 'We can't hold this position all day!'

Anne swallowed hard, and after a moment's fumbling, opened the door. Barry began to pay out the rope ladder. The end of it reached right down to the churning pool. The water splashed all round it, and Barry could even feel the spray on his face as he leant out of the plane.

'Now start climbing down! Fast – and no fumbling! Remember you're on film!'

That was the right thing to say to Barry Bigley. The thought that cameras were trained on him (there was a second camera, he noticed, covering them from the ground) instantly brought out the showman in him. First, he put on a tough, wry Bogart look. Then he managed a mocking Roger Moore smile. Then he started coolly climbing down the ladder. The only trouble was, he was too busy looking at the cameras to notice where he was going. He missed a rung, and slithered almost right down to the bottom . . .

Philip Beatty seemed delighted at the mishap. 'Great stuff!

he bellowed. 'Should give every viewer a thrill! Now, you, Anne –'

Anne was on the ladder, and had climbed half way down it, before anyone could blink. Peter followed, shaking so violently that the ladder swayed from side to side. Kate tried to follow, but the moment she got on the swinging ladder, all her worst fears were realised. She turned green, and started heaving. By closing her eyes, and concentrating furiously on climbing down, she just succeeded in stopping herself from being sick – and to her great astonishment, when she opened her eyes again, she saw Philip Beatty's head popping out through the door of the helicopter above her.

'Relax!' he yelled. 'We just wanted a shot of all four of you on the ladder, having fearlessly climbed out of the plane. We've got it – so we can pack it in now, and go round to the railway for Shot Two. You needn't climb back in the plane. Just carry on down the ladder and we'll drop you at the side of the pool.'

'Th-th-thank you very much,' said Kate.

She stopped heaving – but started slithering, landing heavily on top of Peter, who lost his hold and crashed on Anne, who yelped and toppled on to Barry. The result was a painful four-point landing by all the Dean Street Detectives together on the path beside the pool.

People rushed from all directions to help them up. They included not only the ambulance-men, but also Rosalie Penrose and Bettina Rand, who had both turned up to watch the filming.

'You did very well, dears,' Miss Penrose said, in her usual beaming-headmistress style.

Bettina Rand was looking at Barry with her large eyes glowing. 'You started down that ladder with such an air!' she told him. 'I was reminded of the time I met that dear Paul Newman . . .'

Barry bowed, and looked all set to sign autographs. His

moment of grandeur, though, was rather spoiled by Kate.

'Urgh!' she said, and rushing to the edge of the pool, actually *was* sick – several times over.

13

Steam Scene

Bettina Rand produced a bottle of tablets from her handbag.

'All the great stars suffer from nervous stomachs,' she said. 'Here's something I always carry with me – personally recommended by Marilyn Monroe.'

An ambulance man brought a glass of water. Two tablets were popped in it, and Kate found herself drinking something that tasted like exploding spearmint. It seemed to work, though. In a moment, the sick feeling vanished.

Just then, Philip Beatty's secretary came up with some news that made her feel better still. 'Mrs Miller has just rung us from the hospital. They say that Mr Miller will have to stay there for the night, but will be all right to come home tomorrow. Normally children aren't allowed in the hospital, but the ward sister says she'll make an exception in your case, and you can go and visit him after you leave here. Mr Beatty says he'll arrange for a car. He's also going to have Mr Miller's car taken round to the hospital, so that after your visit, Mrs Miller can drive you all home.'

Beatty himself arrived at that moment.

'That's for when the filming's finished, of course,' he said, glancing down at his watch. 'Which it never will be, if we don't move on soon. The next stop's the Kettlewell Steam Railway. Into the vans again, everybody – please.'

For once he sounded quite good-tempered. It was almost as though the impossible had happened, and he was actually beginning to like the Dean Street Detectives. This time,

Bettina Rand and Rosalie Penrose climbed into the van alongside them, and they, Paddy Reilly and Philip Beatty set off for the railway together.

The Detectives were beginning to forget their fears. After all, the helicopter scene had gone off without anything terrible happening – and here were all the suspects in the case behaving very *un*suspiciously, smiling and even beaming at them.

Only Peter kept remembering that one of the people in the van was almost certain to be the owner of that dangerous name. Somewhere at the back of his mind, he was still restlessly juggling with their initials. B.R., R.P., P.R., P.B. *Which* of them was most likely to have come out on that sheet as P.P.? Until they knew, he told himself, they couldn't afford to relax. Especially not on the Kettlewell Steam Railway . . .

A lot was already going on at the railway station when they arrived. The place would normally have been closed at this time of the year. It was on a branch line that had been shut down by British Rail long years ago, and had been re-opened by the Kettlewell Amateur Railway Society only the previous June. The Society usually ran short trips on Saturdays and Sundays during the summer season, using their one steam locomotive, two coaches and guard's van along about a kilometre of track. Theirs was probably the only railway in the world that didn't actually get anybody anywhere. The train just steamed to the end of the track, and then reversed, puffing cheerfully back along the way it had been. But it gave passengers a chance to take in some beautiful scenery, and experience the thrill of travelling behind a gleaming engine, puffing out great clouds of smoke, that conjured up memories of the Flying Scotsman and all the great thundering giants of the grand old age of steam.

As soon as the Society had heard that Britannia TV

wanted to film their railway, all ten of its members had become greatly excited. That morning, they had turned up at the crack of dawn and had polished their locomotive until every inch of it sparkled in the April sun. The station was not only open; every corner of it had been swept and dusted. Even the metal bridge over the railway line, at the end of one of the platforms, had been scrubbed and polished, so that it sparkled almost as brightly as the train.

Technicians from Britannia TV had also been busy since the early morning. A rope-ladder had been attached to the highest part of the bridge, dangling over the track, and cameras were cleverly mounted above it to film the scene. The train itself was waiting about a hundred metres down the line, already with steam up and raring to go. The engine driver and his stoker, wearing neat blue uniforms obviously straight from the cleaners, bowed and waved as though they were already being filmed.

'Right!' said Philip Beatty, as he and the Dean Street Detectives pushed their way through the throng of onlookers lining the platform. 'Now I'll spell out once again exactly what we're going to do. We've already got a shot of the four of you climbing out of the chopper on to a rope-ladder. This shot is to show you all still clinging to the ladder, with the train passing underneath. We won't be taking the bridge, so all the polishing has been in vain! We want the viewers to assume that you're still hanging from the helicopter, and are about to jump down on the roof of the train. So you've got to look down at the train, as though you're on the point of jumping.'

'But we don't actually jump?' said Kate.

'Not unless you want to break that pretty little neck,' said Philip Beatty heavily. 'No. You just hang there. The train will come thundering past, just below your feet – as far as the cameras are concerned, you'll probably all disappear in a massive cloud of steam. Then we'll be cutting to the next shot

– the one we'll take when we get back to the studio – which will seem to show you landing on the roof of the train. Do you understand now?'

'I – er – think so,' Kate was beginning, but Anne hurriedly cut in. She couldn't stand anyone thinking the Dean Street Detectives dim. 'Of course we do,' she said briskly. 'When do we start?'

'You can take up your positions on the rope-ladder straight away,' Beatty told her. 'Just go up on the bridge, and Paddy will come along with you to help you over the side. Don't forget – you've got to go down the ladder in the same order as in the last shot. Otherwise everyone will wonder how you've changed round. That means Barry goes first, you second, Peter next and Kate last. Okay? Then get cracking – please.' He added the 'please' as an afterthought. He was almost back to barking and snarling the commands.

The four Detectives, with Paddy behind them, walked along the platform and up the steps of the bridge. When they reached the top, it looked a long, long way down to the track below. Even Barry had to swallow hard before he could bring himself to clamber over the rail on to the rope-ladder. And Anne – who hadn't actually a very good head for heights – had to struggle hard to stop herself closing her eyes as she followed him. Peter had a different problem altogether. For a good five seconds, his limbs simply refused to move.

'Absolutely no risks?' he muttered under his breath. This whole thing was beginning to look very risky indeed. It only wanted one strand of that rope-ladder to break – just as the train was passing –

Perhaps fortunately, he was given no more time to think. Paddy Reilly seized him, with the effortlessness of a born wrestler, and the next thing he knew he was over the rail and on that ladder, whether it was safe or not. Above him, Kate was being given the same treatment – protesting with a series of indignant squeals.

'Leave me alone! I can manage! Hey – what – ooo-er . . .'

She was obviously over the edge and on to the ladder now. The whole contraption began swaying from side to side, just as it had done when dangling from the helicopter. His own shaking, Peter remembered, had caused it to do that before . . .

But *then* there had been nothing really to be afraid of. They had been only a couple of metres or so above the churning water of that pool. Now they were much higher up – ten metres, perhaps fifteen, perhaps more. And below them were the hard, hard tracks – shimmering blindingly in the sun –

'I suppose things could be worse,' Peter heard Barry drawling somewhere beneath him. 'Eight-year-old Emma Jane Whatsit might have had us tied to the line! I'd like to meet that young lady sometime. I'll give *her* ideal adventure –'

'Sh!' said Anne urgently. 'There might be a microphone somewhere, picking up everything we say.'

'So what?' Barry answered. 'In the circumstances, who could blame us for – er – letting off steam . . .'

Suddenly there was a shout from Philip Beatty below. Even his voice sounded hollow, echoing, faraway. 'Cue cameras! Action, all of you – here comes the train – look ready to jump . . .'

The rest of his words were lost in a shattering roar of sound as the gleaming locomotive roared on its way. It covered the hundred metres to the bridge in a flash, making the whole station shake as it passed. The bridge shook too – and the rope-ladder seemed to become alive, writhing like a snake in the Dean Street Detectives' fingers as they struggled not to lose hold. Trying desperately to look ready to jump, as requested, all four of them glanced down – and gasped. They had a close-up overhead view of the racing, roaring engine, its funnel gaping at them like an open mouth – the open mouth of a blistering hell.

A blast of heat fanned their faces, turning their cheeks an instant crimson – and then came the steam, a massive, cloud-size billow of it that blotted out everything around, above and beneath them in a clammy, clinging blanket of white. It was so thick that they couldn't see each other's faces – or even their own fingers, arms or shoulders. There was nothing any of them could do except grit their teeth and hang on blindly to the rope-ladder – and suddenly they couldn't even do that.

The combined weight of their struggling bodies proved too much for the ladder, and it abruptly gave way. First the right strand gave and then the left, one straight after the other, with two cracks like revolver shots. Before they could half take in what was happening, the Dean Street Detectives found themselves falling – helplessly falling down through the sea of white towards the sound of the thundering train.

14

'No Risk This Time...'

It was perhaps the most terrifying moment of their lives – but fortunately, the terror was short-lived. Especially for Barry. His toes were dangling less than a metre above the roof of the train, and he landed almost before he knew he was falling.

He came down heavily on all fours, and received painful cracks on both his hands – and both his knees. He had no time to worry about that, though. In the next split seconds, things happened all round him with brain-numbing speed. First, he heard resounding thuds – one beside and two behind him. Then he heard sounds through the all-engulfing whiteness: a gasp in Anne's voice, a groan in Peter's, a choking shriek in Kate's.

'Welcome aboard the Orient Express,' he said hoarsely. 'Have your tickets ready, please –'

He stopped, blinking. The wind rushing past them had whipped the blanket of steam away, and everything was suddenly sharp, clear and in brilliant sunlight. Including the fact that Kate was just about to roll clean off the edge of the rocking, swaying roof. He lunged forward and grabbed her just in time ... just in time to turn his attention to Peter, who had succeeded in standing up but hadn't noticed a swiftly-approaching overhanging tree.

'Duck, for God's sake!' he yelled.

Peter ducked, lost his balance, and fell on Anne, who lost her temper completely.

'That's about the millionth time you've landed on top of me –' she yelled, and then gasped as the brakes were slammed on, and the whole train came to a shuddering halt.

Until the steam had cleared away, no one on the platform had realised what had happened. But now everyone had woken up to the emergency, and their terrified shouts and yells had reached the startled driver of the train. He had brought it to a halt only about fifty metres down the track.

In response to further shouts and signals, he started to reverse the engine – and moving very slowly now, the train steamed back into the station. The Dean Street Detectives remembered to lie flat as it made its return journey under the bridge.

When the train finally stopped, dozens of eager hands reached out to help them down on to the platform. Most of the onlookers imagined they'd been watching a pre-arranged stunt, and there was a spontaneous burst of applause.

Barry, of course, beamed and bowed. 'Thank you, friends,' he said. 'And don't forget you've been watching a genuine Dean Street Detectives adventure . . .'

Anne, on the other hand, was furious. 'In which we could easily all have been killed!' she stormed, glaring at Philip Beatty, who could be seen towering above the crowd.

Beatty gave his usual scornful laugh. 'Killed? What absolute rubbish. You were never in the slightest danger. Not that this wasn't a regrettable accident. There will be a full inquiry, I assure you – *I* shall demand it if no one else does! But meanwhile, we still have one more shot to take, back in the studio on the mock train roof. After your experience on a real one, this should be a walkover for you. This way!'

He marched off down the platform towards the exit – and the waiting van.

Bettina Rand suddenly appeared, with Rosalie Penrose beside her. 'I'm not sure I should trust him, darlings,' Bettina whispered. 'All the great villains can be very convincing when they try. I remember poor dear Boris Karloff saying to me –'

'What *are* you talking about, Bettina?' interrupted Miss Penrose. She looked like a severe headmistress now, not a genial one. 'There are no villains at Britannia TV! Mr Beatty may be a little hard on these children now and then – but I'm quite certain he'd never willingly harm a hair of their heads! Nor would anyone else here. This unfortunate incident must have been just an accident, that's all.'

'Sure and that's right enough, Miss Penrose,' came a jovial Irish voice, as Paddy Reilly joined them. ''Tis terrible sorry I am about the rope-ladder, but it was no one's fault. I've been up to look at it – and it just happened that the ropes were up against a sharp bit of metal on the bridge, and all that swaying and rubbing cut them right in two. No one could have imagined that a thing like that would happen. No, it was definitely no one's fault at all.'

Wasn't it? Peter wondered. It sounded as though someone had been pretty careless to him . . .

Philip Beatty looked round, and was furious to find that the Dean Street Detectives were not behind him. 'This way!' he thundered. 'Unless you've finally lost your famous nerves!' Thinking that perhaps that wasn't the best way to persuade them, he added: 'I can assure you that I will take full charge of this last scene myself. You have my personal guarantee that there will be absolutely no risk at all.'

Very reluctantly, the Dean Street Detectives followed him.

'It's a funny thing,' said Barry, in his most mocking voice, 'but I seem to have heard those words before . . .'

Once they were back at the Britannia TV studios, it turned out that the set wasn't quite ready, so Philip Beatty decided to break for lunch. A couple of hours later, after being treated to a four-course lunch in the staff restaurant, the Dean Street

Detectives found themselves back once more in Studio One. The place had changed a lot since the previous day. There was no sign now of the imitation consulting room; no sign, either, of the mock roofs or the collapsed chimney.

Most of the floor-space was now taken up by a long, snaking imitation train. It was a pretty curious-looking train. There was no engine in front of it, no guard's van behind it and no railway track underneath it. Its four coaches rested on a bed of coiled springs, and were surrounded by a dozen robot-like arms. At a touch of a button, Philip Beatty explained, the coaches would start bouncing up and down on the springs, and the arms would rock them from side to side.

'It's a very realistic action,' he said. 'Of course, the arms and the springs won't show on the TV screen, because as you can see the cameras are focussed on the roofs. The four of you climb up on to that platform –' he pointed to a few rickety-looking planks on some scaffolding near the ceiling '– and jump down on to the top of the train. It'll look as though you're landing from the rope-ladder. Then we'll operate the shaking and rocking machinery, and all you have to do is run along the train roofs from coach to coach. Paddy Reilly – disguised as your masked enemy again – will be on the last of the coaches, with two or three friends. You have to fight them – and hurl them off. We've put mattresses on the floor alongside the last coach, so that no one gets hurt.'

'But what about the first three coaches?' asked Kate. 'Supposing we fall off one of those?'

'You won't,' Beatty said. 'The rocking and shaking will be quite gentle, I promise you. Right. We'll start with a preliminary run-through, I think – and I'll come with you and show you exactly what I want you to do.'

The next moment, he was leading them up a seemingly endless flight of metal steps to the high platform. It was exactly like walking up on to that bridge all over again. Everything looked a long way down – and so did the little group watching them. Bettina, Rosalie, Paddy and several technicians were all standing by below.

'Good luck, darlings,' they heard Bettina call up to them, and she seemed to be actually blowing a kiss at Barry.

'Probably thinks you *are* Paul Newman by now,' said Kate.

'Who can blame her, Katie me darling?' murmured Barry. 'It's such an easy mistake to make.'

'Silence on the set, please!' barked Philip Beatty. 'Cue roof effects!'

Somewhere far below, someone pressed a button – and the train roofs, about two metres below them, began to shake and sway, to the accompaniment of a grinding rumble that seemed to shake the whole platform.

'Doesn't look all that gentle an action to me,' muttered Peter.

'You're just yellow – as usual,' grunted Anne, beside him.

'Right!' said Beatty. 'Now watch me jump – and then I want the four of you to do the same . . .'

He sprang down on to the nearest roof, and seemed to have no trouble standing upright on it. He even managed one of his flashing smiles as he looked up at them and beckoned.

'You see?' he said. 'It's a piece of cake!'

The Dean Street Detectives believed him – and jumped, one after the other. Even Peter was telling himself that there wasn't anything to worry about this time.

He was never more wrong in his life.

15

Shake-Up

Precisely what went wrong with the mechanism, the Dean Street Detectives never discovered. But the moment the four of them followed Philip Beatty on to the roof of the first mock coach, the rocking and shaking accelerated, and turned into a deadly bouncing and jarring. Suddenly the whole roof was behaving like a bucking bronco, springing up and down with such force that within a second, Anne, Peter, Kate and Barry – and Philip Beatty himself – were simply hurled off it, clean into the air.

That could have been nasty – very nasty indeed. There were mattresses round the fourth coach, but not the first one. In this part of the studio, there was nothing to land on but the hard concrete of the studio floor. To come down on that, after being shot high in the air, could result in broken arms, legs, heads or even necks . . .

Beatty came down first, and hardest. He cracked his head on the concrete, and lay, white and very still.

The Dean Street Detectives came down a split-second later – together.

As always in an emergency, they had instinctively closed ranks. The moment he'd realised what was happening, Barry had clutched Kate's arm, Peter had seized Anne's, and Anne had grabbed Barry's. None of them could have explained quite why they did it – but this bunching together very probably saved their lives. Individually, they would have been shot by the powerful springs to almost ceiling height. Together, their combined weight – which amounted to under 160 kilos – kept them low, so that they had little further than the height of the mock coach to fall. And since they fell on top of each other, only the Detective at the bottom landed on the concrete floor with maximum force.

That happened to be Barry, the toughest fighter at Dean Street Comprehensive – who was so used to taking tumbles that he did the best thing possible. He relaxed all his muscles, kept his head well forward, and landed bruised, shaken and totally winded – but otherwise okay.

None of the others had even a scratch, although Anne cracked her head against Peter's, and was literally seeing red – a red mist swimming in front of her eyes that made it hard for her to see straight, or think straight either. Not that a little thing like that ever stopped Anne, when she was really angry. She picked herself up, strode across to Philip Beatty's prone body, and shouted, at the top of her voice:

'How many *more* accidents are you going to allow to happen during this show? Isn't it *ever* going to dawn on you that someone's trying to murder –'

She stopped, gasping, as the mist cleared and she suddenly realised that Philip Beatty couldn't hear her. His face was deathly white, in startling contrast to that jet black beard. His eyes were closed, and his breathing was so hoarse that it sounded like groaning. As she dropped down on one knee beside him, trying hard to remember what she knew about first aid, alarm bells started ringing all over the studio. Bettina, Rosalie and Paddy Reilly came hurrying across.

'Don't touch him,' Miss Penrose warned. 'The ambulance-men will be here in a moment.'

As always, it seemed, at Britannia TV, thought Peter grimly. He was hurriedly revising his ideas. Up to that moment, Philip Beatty had really been his Suspect Number One. But surely, he wouldn't have arranged an 'accident' involving himself – unless he was trying a very reckless double bluff. Who, then, was their secret enemy?

Beatty was now beginning to recover. His breathing became normal. His eyes opened. And suddenly he was struggling to his feet, and glaring round him.

'What – what happened?' he asked.

Before anyone could tell him, he'd remembered.

'Oh, yes, of course – the rocking mechanism went wrong.'

'Wrong?' said Kate. 'It went berserk, bonkers – bananas –'

She searched for another word, and Anne supplied it. 'It became very, very dangerous, Mr Beatty,' she said. 'And we think someone intended it to be just that.'

'Oh, rubbish,' said Beatty. 'It was just a little accident. None of you children look badly hurt to me. Well, then, what are you complaining about? Let's – let's get on with the scene.'

'Without fixing the machinery?' gasped Anne.

'What do you think we are?' said Barry. 'The Dean Street Flying Circus?'

Beatty realised that he'd gone too far this time. He put a hand to his forehead. It came away wet with perspiration. 'Of course I didn't mean without fixing the machinery,' he said. 'We'll all take ten while the technicians check it out.'

'It'll take more than ten minutes, I'm afraid, Mr Beatty,' a technician called out. The man was down on his knees below the mock train, inspecting the damage. 'This'll need a complete overhaul. Could take the rest of the day.'

'And so I should think!' said Rosalie Penrose severely. 'The very idea of risking these children's lives – just to finish quickly, and keep inside a budget!'

It was probably the first time she'd criticised the producer to his face – no one was more fiercely loyal to Britannia TV. Beatty rounded on her, looking astonished, half-dazed. Before he could reply, Bettina Rand sailed into the attack.

'You're as heartless as any of those terrible old German directors with their monocles, and revolvers and hunting-crops, who used to call everybody "Schweinhunds". Don't you realise what these children have been through? In the past few hours, they've seen their father nearly killed by a falling crate, and dragged off in an ambulance. They've had a rope-ladder break under them and been thrown on top of a charging train. Now they've been sent flying by a crazy machine – and all you can say is "What are you making a fuss about? Let's get on with the scene." Honestly, darling – anyone would think you *hated* children . . .'

She broke off abruptly.

Beatty, under attack from all sides, was suddenly not only sweating – but swaying. 'That's a lie. I don't hate children. I only hate kids who – who think they're cleverer than I am.'

'Why?' said Bettina tensely. '*Because you feel inside that they may be right?*'

Beatty didn't reply. He just pulled himself together with a great effort and barked: 'That's all for today, everyone. We'll start again early tomorrow morning. Meanwhile kids, I'll arrange for a car to come and take you home.'

'We were going to be taken to Kettlewell Hospital to see Dad,' said Anne.

'Eh? Oh, yes. Well, I'll see that it stops there for half an hour or so on the way. Meanwhile – thanks for all your efforts. Bettina's right – you have had a lot to put up with. And you've taken it very well.' Suddenly he managed that flashing smile. 'You could say you've passed *my* personal test!' he finished, and half-stalked, half-staggered out.

The Dean Street Detectives stared after him, very puzzled. They never thought the moment would come when they'd get praise from Philip Beatty.

'Amazing what a bang on the head will do to people,' said Barry.

'Ye-es,' said Peter. 'If he's not just acting . . .'

He still wasn't sure whether to cross Beatty off his list of suspects – or keep him right at the top.

Bettina was suddenly beaming at them.

'Darlings,' she said. 'After the star performance you've given today, you deserve to go home like stars. So I'm going to lend you my Rolls – and its chauffeurs, of course.'

'Chauffeurs?' gasped Kate. 'You mean – you've got two?'

'That's right,' said Bettina. 'One to drive, and one to pop in and out doing errands . . . I know you want to go to the hospital, but that suits me fine. I feel I ought to pay a visit there myself, to see how poor dear David Reynolds is getting on. We'll all drive there together. Then you can come to my house for some tea and cakes. Then I'll get my two men to drive you home. How does that sound?'

'Fine,' chorused the Detectives together. Arriving home in Fenton in a Rolls, behind two uniformed chauffeurs, wouldn't make a bad end to what had been a pretty shattering day.

Five minutes later, they were sitting at the back of the Rolls – quite the largest and most sumptuous car they'd ever been in – with the chauffeurs in the front, and Bettina herself sitting beside them. She had a large black handbag on her lap – so vast that it was almost the size of a weekend case. Obviously the thing had cost a fortune, thought Peter. The clasp looked as though it was made of polished silver, and the initials BR were picked out in sparkling jewels.

The star was still smiling, but there was an odd look on her face now – and her large eyes were narrowed almost like Peter's.

'Now I'll tell you the real reason why I wanted you to use my car,' she said. 'With all the strange things that have been going on, I realised that it was the only way to make sure that no more nasty little accidents happened to you today. Kettlewell Hospital, Jules!' she called out to the uniformed man behind the wheel. Then she ordered his companion: 'And Martin, keep a look out behind and let me know the moment you suspect we are being followed.'

Peter's own eyes were wide now – with astonishment.

Bettina laughed.

'Don't look so surprised, darlings. I played a woman detective for years and years on American TV, and I've become pretty good at deducing things. It's obvious that someone is trying to kill all four of you – and poor dear David and your father too.' She glanced down at her watch. 'It'll take us five minutes to reach that hospital. In that time, if we put our heads together, I'm sure we can work out just who that someone can be.'

16

Who's Doing It?

'It's just like a whodunit, isn't it?' Bettina went on. 'Or rather a who's-doing-it. Because he or she hasn't finished yet – and is almost certain to try again.'

'Thanks very much,' said Kate hoarsely. 'That's just the cheery thought we needed.'

'There's no point in not facing facts, dear,' Bettina told her. 'And it's not a good idea to *hide* facts from each other, either. Part of being a good detective is keeping one's eyes open, and I noticed David Reynolds taking Peter aside and having a long talk with him yesterday. Now, Peter, tell me straight. Did David say anything to you about having a deadly enemy?'

Peter was looking even more startled.

'Er. Well. Yes, he did,' he admitted.

Bettina nodded.

'I thought as much. He told me the other night that his life was being threatened – but I couldn't get him to say who was threatening it. Did he, by any chance, tell *you*?'

'Um. Well. Er . . .' Peter was finding it very difficult to know what to say.

'Come on,' Bettina urged. 'You might as well tell me. Because one thing's for sure, darling. The *enemy* believes that you know his – or her – name. Nothing else explains these repeated attempts on all your lives.'

Peter decided, at last, to be frank. 'Well, the enemy's wrong,' he said. 'David Reynolds *was* going to tell me the name. In fact, he scribbled it down on his clipboard. But then he changed his mind, screwed up the sheet and pocketed it. All I could get hold of was the sheet underneath.'

Bettina nodded approvingly. 'Ah, yes. The old Sherlock Holmes trick. If David had pressed hard enough with his pencil, the name would have come through on that. Well? Had it come through?'

Peter hesitated once again. Anne decided to answer for him.

'No, it hadn't, Miss Rand. At least, not properly. All we could make out was what looked like two capital Ps with a funny line between them.'

Bettina's eyes widened. 'Two capital Ps? But there's nobody in the studio with a name that would fit that.'

Kate suddenly sailed in. 'Peter had a theory that some of the strokes may be missing on the second sheet. He reckons that the Ps could originally have been Rs or Bs. In other words –'

Barry didn't see why he should be left out of the conversation either. 'In other words,' he murmured, 'the situation becomes very interesting, because the name could have been Philip Beatty.'

'Or Rosalie Penrose,' said Anne.

'Or Paddy Reilly,' said Kate. 'Or –'

She broke off hurriedly, leaving it to Peter to blurt out, awkwardly: 'Or. Well. Um. We reckoned it might even just be – er – Bettina Rand.'

The famous film star wasn't in the least taken aback. In fact, she burst out laughing. 'So I've been on your list of suspects, have I? What fun, darlings. I've acted three times in Agatha Christie spin-off movies, you know. Once I *was* the fiendish villainess at the end. I was *so* pleased. I had to do a marvellous "You'll-never-take-me-alive-Inspector" scene, and take poison with a massive thunderstorm in the background . . . But I must say, the other names on your list do seem a *trifle* more likely than poor little me!'

By that time, the Dean Street Detectives were laughing too.

'Just a trifle,' Barry agreed. 'I'm betting myself that it's Philip Beatty. He looks like a villain. He acts like one. And he's the producer and director of the whole show, so could easily have arranged – or ordered somebody to arrange – all these "accidents". I know he got himself hurt in the last of them, but that could have been just to throw us off the scent. He was keen enough to send us straight into danger all over again – and probably would have done, if you hadn't stopped him, Miss Rand.'

'I always like to do what I can for hero-types, darling,' said Bettina, giving him a melting look from those famous large eyes.

'Huh!' said Kate. 'My money's on that Paddy Reilly. He was in charge of all the special effects, remember. And there's something about him that gives me the shivers. What's more,' she added, as though that settled the matter, 'I'm not even sure he's really Irish.'

'Don't forget Rosalie Penrose,' said Anne. 'She keeps in the background, I know – and she pretends to be very friendly, but secretly, I think she hates us. She gave that away long ago – when she twisted her ankle on that roof.'

Kate groaned. 'Let's face it,' she said. 'It could be any of them. And we just haven't a clue which it is.'

Bettina turned to Peter. 'That piece of paper you talked about. Have you still got it with you, darling? If so, could you let me see it? It's just possible that I might spot something you didn't. It's not likely, I know, seeing that you've such a brilliant detective brain. But –'

Peter reached into his pocket, and pulled out the sheet. It was crumpled now, and some of the fingerprint powder had rubbed off. But it was still possible to make out the two Ps and the line between them:

$$P \longrightarrow P$$

Just as he was about to hand the paper over, Peter glanced down at it again himself – and suddenly gave a violent start. He had always felt that there was a clue there somewhere which he hadn't spotted – and now suddenly it was blindingly clear. He didn't look at the two Ps this time, but at the line between them. No one would make a straight line like that when writing a name – *unless underlining it or crossing a T*. That line was too high up to be underlining anything, so it had to mean that the first name had a T in it. Probably two Ts, as it was such a long name. And there was no T in Philip, Rosalie or Paddy, Peter realised . . . only in Bett –

That was the moment when the film star snatched the piece of paper out of his hand. It was a violent, vicious snatch, and looking up, he suddenly saw a lot that was both violent and vicious in those million-dollar eyes.

'You know, don't you?' Bettina Rand said softly.

Peter swallowed hard. Acting wasn't his strong point, any more than action was. He started mumbling 'Ers' and 'Wells' but Bettina interrupted him.

'I'm very sorry, darlings,' she murmured. 'More sorry than I can say. You'd all of you just convinced me that David Reynolds *hadn't* given you my name, after all – and that I was wrong in trying to harm you. But now, I'm afraid –'

She broke off, and glanced out of the window.

'Ah, we're outside the hospital. Pull up at the main gates, Jules, I'm getting out. Martin – make sure these children don't get out too. And after I've gone, take care of them – *for good . . .*'

Her voice was as husky as usual, but now so loaded with menace that it felt as though a glacial wind was suddenly blowing through the car.

Jules pulled up as he'd been told. Clutching her jewelled handbag, Bettina was out in a flash, slamming the door behind her. In that same instant, the man beside the driver turned round in his seat. He turned awkwardly, because he was wearing a seat-belt – but that didn't stop a revolver appearing as if by magic in his hand.

He didn't look at all like a chauffeur – much more like a gangster of the lowest and deadliest type. His eyes were cold, hard, snake-like ... the eyes of a hired gunman, or even a hired killer.

The sort of man, the Dean Street Detectives told themselves, who really *would* 'take care of them – for good ...'

17

Another Little Accident

The Rolls swept away from the kerb, and the tall, grey hospital building disappeared behind them. The detectives noticed that only out of the corners of their eyes. Most of their attention was focussed on the gun poking at them over the back of the front seat.

Behind it, the gunman smiled crookedly.

'Surprised, kids? You wouldn't be if you knew Bettina like Jules and I do. We've been working for her for twenty years or more – and we could tell you things about her that would make your hair curl. All through her career, everyone who's got in her way, a rival actress, say, or a producer who turns her down for a part, has always had a nasty accident shortly afterwards. No one can ever prove anything against her, because anybody who gets any proof meets with a nasty accident too!'

'But how does she arrange all these accidents?' Anne asked.

'That's easy. She's not a big star any more, but she's still got enough money to bribe people with. And she always knows just who to bribe. You'd probably find that half-a-dozen of the technicians on the studio floor are in her pay, for a start. And look at the result. David Reynolds starts to suspect her. Next thing you know, a chimney's fallen on him – and he's in intensive care.' The man's smile became so crooked it was positively evil. 'And now that Bettina's paying him a little visit, you can bet he'll be getting *very* intensive care,' he added.

'Just – just what do you mean?' asked a shaken Peter.

'I mean – I don't think she'll be going in there to blow him a kiss, do you?' the man said. 'But don't bother your head about David Reynolds, kids. You've got enough worrying to do about yourselves. Don't forget, I'm under orders to take care of you – for good. That means we'll have to arrange another little accident, involving all of you.'

He turned the nozzle of the gun on to each of them in turn – a puzzling Peter, an angry Kate, a defiant Anne, and finally a cool and mocking Barry. A bewildered look crossed his face. Kids facing a loaded gun, and being threatened with certain death, ought to be panicking, shaking in their shoes. Why weren't these? He didn't realise just how many times the Dean Street Detectives had looked down the nozzles of loaded guns before – or how swiftly they'd turned the tables on the villains behind them . . .

Still having no idea what he was up against, he laughed thickly, sneeringly. 'Yes, that's what's needed, isn't it?' he said. 'Another little accident. Any suggestions?'

'What I'd like to suggest,' said Barry, with a charming smile, 'is that you belt up, you murdering creep.'

Anne, who was sitting beside Barry, felt his elbow giving her a sharp jab on the word 'belt'. It didn't take her more than a tenth of a second to realise what he meant.

By turning right round to level his gun at them, the gangster had placed quite a strain on his seat belt. Its straps were giving out loud creaks as they struggled to hold in his bulky body. The belt's release catch was on the floor betwen the Rolls's two front seats, very close to Anne's toes. All she had to do was lean forwards slightly and press that catch – and the straps would spring loose. With any luck, the gangster would lose his balance, and there would be a moment when the gun would waver, and point at the car roof or the floor. If Barry seized that moment to knock it flying out of his hands . . .

The gunman stared at Barry as if he couldn't believe his ears.

'Don't you talk back at me, kid – or I'll make *you* belt up – forever!' he snarled. He jabbed the gun forward angrily in Barry's direction, his finger turning frighteningly white around the trigger.

There wasn't a second to waste, thought Anne. With all this talk about belts, at any moment their plan might suddenly dawn on him.

Anne never wasted time doing anything, anyway.

Hardly pausing to take a breath, she suddenly stooped down, and . . .

'Hey! What are you playing at, girlie?' shouted the gunman. 'What – *aaah*!'

What seemed like a million things happened at once.

With a resounding *ping*, the released straps sprang loose – and the gunman found himself flying backwards. The gun didn't just waver. It swivelled sideways – and went off in his hands. A bullet whanged across the car, shaving the driver's neck and smashing through the window beside him. The startled driver, winged by the bullet, covered in a shower of falling glass, wouldn't have been human if he hadn't turned his head.

It was a bad mistake to make, though.

'Jules!' screamed the gunman. 'Look out, for God's sake! You've gone on the kerb –'

That was the last thing the gunman said for a very long time.

The Rolls had not only mounted the kerb; it was headed for a concrete lamp standard. Jules swung the wheel in a desperate effort to avoid it – but he was seconds too late. The Rolls hit the standard full on. There was a resounding, shuddering, bone-jarring crash. The elegant Rolls-Royce statuette on the bonnet went flying – and so did all the occupants of the car.

Jules, held in by his seat belt, didn't fly far. But his chest fetched up against the steering wheel, his nose hit the dashboard, and he slumped forward, shaken, winded, gasping. Martin the gunman really travelled. The slackened straps were still round him, and stopped him sailing backwards through the windscreen – just. But his head cracked against it, and he fell across the front seat, unconscious.

The Dean Street Detectives found themselves flying too, but only towards the backs of the two front seats – which were so luxuriously upholstered that it was not a lot worse than banging their heads against pillows. They ended in their usual four-way human pile-up on the floor.

For a moment, Peter, Anne and Barry were too bemused to speak. Kate was bemused too, but that didn't stop her speaking.

'How many more times today are we going to get shot, hurled, banged, crashed, thumped, crunked, thwirled – er – zonked – er –'

She gave up, groaning, as accidentally or on purpose, Anne's foot landed in her face.

Barry was recovering now. From somewhere at the bottom of the pile, he reached out a long arm and unfastened the nearest door. The Dean Street Detectives half-crawled, half-tumbled out into the street. It was a sleezy-looking back street, they noticed. No one seemed to be about. But the crash must have been heard; any second, people would come running.

The Detectives decided to start running, too, or at any rate, to try to run. All any of them could manage was a shaky stagger.

'We must get to the hospital,' Anne stuttered. 'Whatever Bettina's planning to do to David, we've got to – stop it –'

'If we're not too late,' breathed Peter.

They took one more glance back at the crashed Rolls. Martin was recovering now. His face could be glimpsed through the window as he peered blearily out. Barry waved a friendly farewell. Shaken though he was, he could still manage a mocking laugh as he shouted: 'You were quite right, pal. Another little accident was *just* what was needed...'

18

Very Intensive Care

Martin groped around dazedly for his gun. Long before he found it, the Dean Street Detectives were streets away, heading for Kettlewell Hospital.

They knew which direction to take. Although they had only glimpsed the hospital out of the corners of their eyes, they had noticed its gaunt, tower-like shape, and now they could see it in the distance, rearing above all the buildings in between.

Peter, for once, took the lead. He had a talent for finding his way around a strange neighbourhood, although Anne made it difficult for him to use it by hissing: 'Get a move on!' every time he paused. Finally he lost his temper, and barked back: 'All right, dear sister, I *will* get a move on – but don't blame me if we wind up down some blind alley or at the bottom of a river!'

He shot off down a side turning, and the next second was zig-zagging his way through a car park, with the other three blundering along behind.

'Where on earth do you think you're going?' grumbled Kate. 'I'll bet this is nowhere near the hospital –'

'Now that's a bet I'd take you up on any time, Katie,' said Barry softly, and he pointed to a sign just ahead of them. It said: *Kettlewell Hospital Car Park. For Doctors and Nursing Staff Only*. Close to the sign was a door, labelled: *Casualties, Emergencies, Intensive Care*.

'Right,' said Anne, briskly. 'Well done, Peter. We've arrived!'

'Let's just hope we're in time,' said Peter.

'Of course we are!' said Kate. 'When you come to think about it, David Reynolds can't be in any real danger. In Intensive Care Units they have nurses checking on the patients every few minutes. And apart from that, don't you remember? Mr Miller arranged with the Kettlewell Inspector for a policeman to be posted right outside David's ward. Even Bettina couldn't get past all that!'

'Couldn't she?' said Peter. 'I wonder.'

'Why waste time wondering?' snapped his sister. 'Let's find out – *now*!'

She went charging through the door, the others behind her; walked straight up to the first nurse she saw, and demanded: 'Show us the way, please, to Intensive Care.'

She'd picked the wrong person to approach. The nurse was clearly a sister, or maybe a matron, and wasn't going to be ordered about by impertinent schoolkids.

'Show you the way to Intensive Care, indeed!' she barked. 'Children are not allowed to visit any part of this hospital – least of all, *that* unit! You will leave at once, all four of you! At once, I say –'

Peter groaned. There were times, he told himself, when Anne had about as much sense as a charging rhinoceros.

Aloud, he said, very politely: 'Good afternoon, sister. We don't want to visit the unit, but we would like to speak to the policeman on duty there. We have an urgent message for him from our father, Detective Superintendent Miller –'

It was an unlikely story, but it was all he could think of. And to his surprise, it worked wonders. Children who asked to see policemen must be law-abiding, the sister reckoned – and she was suddenly all smiles. 'Oh, you want to speak to Constable Anderson, do you? Right. Well, wait here and I'll get him for you.' She went off down a long corridor, and about a minute later, a heavy, glowering constable appeared.

'What's all this rubbish you've been talking, kids? How can you have a message for me from Detective Superintendent Miller? Mr Miller's in the hospital himself – Ward A1 –'

Peter couldn't think what to say. Anne took over.

'The message isn't really from our father, it's from us – the Dean Street Detectives,' she said, grimly. 'And it's a very urgent message indeed.' She put on her official police manner, copied from Mr Miller himself. 'We have reason to believe that the man you're guarding, Mr Reynolds, is in very grave danger.'

The constable blinked – and then grinned.

'The police have reason to believe that too, love,' he said, folding his arms. 'That's why I'm here. But don't you worry. No harm's come to him so far, and no harm will – not while I'm here. You go home and forget all about it.'

Kate decided to have a go. 'But you don't understand!' she shouted. 'The killer's here – now – in this hospital! We – we watched her come in –'

'Her?' said the constable.

'Yes!' said Kate, now very worked up. 'It's a woman – a famous one – Bettina Rand –'

That, of course, was the worst thing she could have said. The constable burst out laughing. 'Bettina Rand, the film star? Why, I've been a fan of hers since I was your age! Pull the other leg, kids. It's got bells on it. You're a bit late with all this stuff, anyway – April Fools Day was ten days ago. And now, if you'll excuse me, I must be getting back.'

He wouldn't hear another word from them, but turned and strode off down the corridor. He was chuckling so loudly, and his boots made such a clatter on the tiled floor, that he never noticed the Dean Street Detectives keeping right behind him. They were still behind him when he went through a door marked 'Intensive Care', and stopped outside another door, which had a glass panel in it.

112

There was a chair beside this second door, with a folded newspaper lying on it. Obviously this was where Constable Anderson sat all through the day. He was just about to sit down there again when he decided to take a look at the patient he was guarding. He went up to the door, and squinted through the glass. Suddenly Constable Anderson definitely wasn't laughing. He turned white, and without a word, rushed off to get help.

The Dean Street Detectives crept up to the window and looked through. What they saw made them feel cold all over and sick with dread. On the other side was a bed, with a patient lying in it whom they could just recognise as David Reynolds. And he was obviously in a bad way. The sheets had been ripped clean off the bed. An oxygen mask had been snatched from his face, and was lying beside him. His cheeks were blue, his eyes were wide and sightless, his mouth sagged open, and there was no sign of breath or movement in his body.

'Oh, God,' breathed Peter. 'We are too late. He *has* been given – very intensive care . . .'

A few seconds later, the constable was back, bringing with him a small array of doctors and nurses.

The Dean Street Detectives drew back along the corridor – but they needn't have bothered. No one had any time to notice them. The doctors and nurses rushed through the glass-panelled door, with the constable behind them. When the Detectives crept back, and peered through the glass, all they could see were people bending over the bed, and all they could hear was the hiss of oxygen and a thumping noise, suggesting that David Reynold's chest was being given a pounding massage.

Whatever the treatment was, it worked like magic.

The next time the Detectives peeped through the glass,

Reynolds was propped up against the pillows, his face red now, not blue, his eyes alert and glancing round him fearfully.

'*She* was here,' he kept saying. '*She* was here . . . bending over me . . .'

'He must mean the nurse who came in to see him a few minutes before I was called away,' said the constable. 'Grey-haired, she was . . . tall, with thick spectacles –'

'There's no one here answering *that* description,' a sister told him curtly. 'All the nurses in this unit are young. You should never have let this person in.'

The constable frowned and rubbed his chin. 'How was I to know? She was wearing the full hospital uniform –'

He was obviously completely bewildered. So, for a moment, were the Dean Street Detectives. Bettina Rand's hair, though probably heavily tinted, hadn't the slightest trace of grey. And where could she have got a nurse's uniform from, anyway?

Then Peter remembered. 'Oh, of course,' he said. 'That jewelled handbag – it was nearly as big as a weekend case. She could have packed a complete uniform in there easily – and a load of wigs and disguises, too. Don't forget – she is an actress. I suppose you could say – one of the most famous actresses in the world!'

'Huh!' said Kate. 'One of the corniest, you mean! I used to be knocked out by her old films – when I was eight or nine. But looking back on them now, honestly, she was terrible! How she ever became a film star I'll never know.'

'But we *do* know, Katie me darling,' breathed Barry. 'It happened by accident. Dozens of deliberately arranged, very nasty accid . . .'

He broke off. David Reynolds was talking again.

'Nurse?' he was saying. 'It – it wasn't a nurse. She – she couldn't disguise that evil face from me. It was – Bettina. Bettina Rand. And while she's in this hospital, no one's safe.

No one who knows her secret – or who she thinks might ever discover it . . .'

The nurses and doctors surrounding the bed stared down at their patient, startled. 'Bettina Rand?' one of the doctors said. 'He must be delirious.'

'It's a funny thing, though, sir,' muttered Constable Anderson. 'But I was talking to a group of children in the corridor just now. *They* were warning me about Bettina Rand. I thought they were joking . . .'

'Children?' said the sister severely. 'In this hospital? That's strictly forbidden . . .'

She glanced up at that moment – and saw the four Dean Street Detectives staring at her through the glass door. What happened next in there the Detectives never knew. Something told them it was time to leave.

They rushed off down the corridor the way they had come, Kate grumbling furiously. 'They have the most dangerous woman in Britain loose around the hosptial, and all they worry about is *us*.'

The others were too busy running to talk – until they reached the big swing doors that led out into the car park. Then, just as they were going through them, Peter came out with his favourite line.

'Wait a minute,' he said.

The others stopped, panting. Kate was still grumbling. 'What for, for heaven's sake?' she demanded. Then she remembered. 'Oh, of course. We haven't seen Dad.'

'That's right,' said Peter. Suddenly he looked very grim and tense. 'And I think we should see him quick.'

'Why quick?' said Anne.

'Remember what David Reynolds said,' Peter told her. 'No one here is safe who knows Bettina's secret – *or who she thinks might ever discover it*. And I've just realised who that includes. Bettina probably believes that we told Dad all about our investigations – and that we showed him that "P –

P" clue. "If the kids can work out that it spells Bettina Rand," she'll say to herself, "so can he". And don't forget she believes that she's got rid of the four of us – and David Reynolds too. From her point of view, that's bound to make Dad her one remaining danger . . .'

Anne suddenly looked as grim and tense as her brother.

'And if she could get into Intensive Care with that uniform,' she said softly, 'she'll have no trouble with Dad's ward – A1. It's just an ordinary ward – and these are visiting hours, too, when anybody can come in . . .'

She stopped there, sudden horror tightening her throat so that she couldn't even say, 'Let's go'.

19

A1 Emergency

Not that Anne needed to say it. All four of them were already charging back down the hospital corridor. At the end was a lift, marked: 'FLOORS 1–20. WARDS A1–17.'

The lift was already standing at the ground floor. They got in, and Anne pressed a button marked: 'FLOOR 20 – WARD A1'.

'The ward we want *would* be right at the top,' groaned Kate.

Hours seemed to go by as the lift glided upwards past floor after floor: nightmare hours during which all the Detectives kept thinking about David Reynolds, and what Bettina had done to him. Would they find Mr Miller lying unconscious, blue-faced, dying or worse – dead . . .

'She couldn't have done all that much to him,' Kate muttered. 'Not with Mum beside his bed, and all the visitors there and everything. *Could* she?'

Peter was about to point out that there were no limits to what a villainess disguised as a nurse could do, even during visiting hours. But he decided to keep quiet and a second later, they arrived at the twentieth floor. The Dean Street Detectives shot out of the lift, and through some swing doors marked 'Ward A1.'

They found themselves staring at a busy, crowded scene. The ward was a large one, with ten beds down each side. In most of the beds patients were sitting up and talking to visitors, and the sound of cheerful chatter filled the air. To add to the bustle, a white-coated lady from the Hospital League of Friends was wheeling a trolley up and down the middle of the room, serving both patients and visitors with cakes and tea.

Kate felt her spirits rising. With all these people about, and all this cheery bustle, surely Mr Miller couldn't have been . . .

At that moment, Peter spotted his father.

'There's Dad. Last bed on the left, at the very end, with Mum sitting beside – oh, my God!'

'What is it?' said Anne. Peter had gone as white as a hospital bed sheet.

She, Kate and Barry looked the way he was pointing – and suddenly their faces went almost the same colour. They could all see Mr Miller now, but he couldn't see them because he was lying on his side, facing away from them. And he was in no position to turn round. A nurse was standing over him. A tall nurse with grey hair and thick spectacles.

They couldn't see much else about her, except that she had a hypodermic syringe in her hand, and looked as though she was just about to inject something into his arm.

The Dean Street Detectives thought faster than they had ever done before in their lives. There was no point in shouting and screaming. Even if Mr Miller heard them, he wouldn't be able to do anything in the split second before that needle jabbed into him. Their only hope was to *get to him* – but how could they? They'd have to rush past nine beds, and apart from that, there was the tea trolley blocking their way.

The tea trolley. Anne and Barry had the same thought together – and before they knew it, were recklessly charging forwards. No one was standing near the trolley; the white-coated assistant was over by one of the beds handing a patient a cup of tea. So there was no one to stop Anne and Barry as they seized hold of one end of the trolley, and sent it careering slantwise down the aisle towards the foot of Mr Miller's bed.

Fortunately, it was on large rubber wheels which slid like lightning over the ward's highly polished floor. Almost before anyone realised what was happening, it had crashed into the end of the bed. Cups cascaded everywhere, and so did cakes, biscuits, buns . . .

The attendant screamed: 'Help! Hooligans! Vandals!'

Mrs Miller jumped up from her chair, gasping. A startled Mr Miller heaved himself up on one shoulder, and turned round to see what was going on. He saw the children, and his thunderous voice burst through all other sounds like a foghorn scattering seagulls.

'What the devil are you four playing at? What do you mean by charging in here and . . .'

Anne's voice could be pretty thunderous, too, when she wanted it to be – and she did now. 'That nurse, Dad,' she yelled. 'Don't let her – touch you . . .'

Mr Miller stopped roaring. His trained police senses never missed much – and even though he'd turned his back on the nurse, he knew she'd given a violent start. It was a good job that needle had still been several centimetres from his arm, he thought. Otherwise he'd have got a very nasty jab indeed . . .

He turned back to look at her – and saw that she was no longer anywhere near him. The syringe had dropped from her hand, and she was backing away towards the door at the far end of the ward. Not that that would do her much good, he thought grimly. He'd heard it was an emergency exit, leading only to the roof.

He began to notice other things about her. That grey hair was at a peculiar angle. It looked like a wig. And there was something strangely familiar about those eyes behind the spectacles . . .

'Who is this woman?' he roared. 'And just what has she been trying to do to me?'

Kate answered, in an angry voice that rose to a shriek.

'Don't you recognise her? She's the famous Bettina Rand. But don't let that fool you. In the last hour, she's been trying to kill first us, then David Reynolds, and now you. And she's probably murdered dozens of people in her time. People who've found out that she's evil – maybe the most evil woman in the world!'

It was quite a speech – spoken in such a piercing tone that no one in the ward could help hearing every word. A total silence fell on the whole place. Everybody – patients and visitors alike – turned to look at the grey-haired woman in nurse's uniform backing towards the door. Even the tea-lady stopped screaming about what had happened to her trolley, and joined in the staring.

'That hooligan girl is right!' she whispered, awed. 'Take off the wig and the spectacles and it *is* Bettina Rand . . .'

'*Bettina* . . .'

'*Bettina Rand* . . .'

The name seemed suddenly to be coming from all directions, as people whispered it to each other in every part of the room. Then came other whispers, as the rest of what Kate had said sank in.

'Evil?'

'Murderess?'

'Tried to kill? . . .'

Bettina herself was standing as if frozen to the spot, her back to the door. Her wig was more askew than ever, and her spectacles had slipped to the very end of her nose. In the ordinary way, the effect would have been funny, but nobody felt like laughing. They were silenced by the terrifying expression in her eyes – a look of naked hate and fury seldom seen on any human face.

Over and over again, Bettina Rand had killed to stop the public suspecting the truth about her. Now this stupid girl had shouted that truth to the whole ward, there was no way to stop rumours and whispers spreading all over the town, then all over Britain, then all over the world.

There was no way to stop it – but there was one thing she *could* do. And that was to take revenge . . .

Suddenly – so unexpectedly that it took the other Dean Street Detectives totally by surprise – Bettina dashed forwards, grabbed Kate by the arm, and dragged her towards the emergency exit. With her left hand, she was suddenly waving a revolver.

'Don't try to follow, darlings,' she warned Peter, Anne and Barry. Her voice was not just husky now; it was as harsh and grating as though she had a throat full of broken glass. 'Or you'll find that your little friend was right to call me – the most evil woman in the world.'

She went out, still dragging the struggling Kate, and the door behind her closed with a heavy metallic clang.

20

Roof Chase – for Real

Barry reached the door before the echoes of that clang had died away. He opened it and strolled through as coolly as though going for a stroll in the park. Anne and Peter were only a few paces behind him. But before they reached the door Mrs Miller shouted 'Stop!' and Mr Miller yelled:

'Stop! Don't you realise – there's just the roof through there, and we're twenty storeys up! You can't tackle a maniac woman with a gun in a place like that. Come back. Come back, both of you! Wait for me –'

The Detective Superintendent's roar was commanding – but his struggle to get out of bed was pathetic. His right leg hadn't yet been put in plaster. It was still in a tightly bandaged splint, and he couldn't move it an inch. The sweat stood out on his forehead as he made the effort.

'Wait!' he still thundered. 'I'll get help – some of the people here – the police . . . '

'Please listen to him,' Mrs Miller added beseechingly. 'Just this once – please listen.'

Anne hadn't time to argue any more. 'Don't worry, Dad – or you, Mum,' she said briskly. 'Roof chases are our speciality, according to Britannia TV. Come on, Peter.'

She and her brother rushed for the door – but were stopped again, this time by a sound from above their heads. It was a piercing scream – unmistakably Kate's. But it was like no other scream that they had ever heard. It went on and on – a long wail of terror.

Anne and Peter stared at each other, stunned by the same thought.

It was the sort of scream someone would make who was falling from a great height . . . like twenty storeys.

Anne and Peter weren't stunned for long. In half a second, they had crashed open the door together, and were racing, side by side, up a short flight of steps that led straight out on to the roof.

When they reached it, they both gave the same gasp – it was almost a sob – of relief.

Apart from a battered-looking chimney stack in the centre the roof was completely flat. It was also very dangerous. There was no sign of a ridge round the edge of it. If you didn't look where you were going, you could easily step right off it, with nothing to stop you falling three hundred metres to the pavement far, far below.

This, though, had definitely not happened to Kate. She was still very much on the roof, and still letting out that long, bloodcurdling wail.

One glance – and Anne and Peter could see why.

Bettina Rand was standing about halfway between the chimney and the left-hand edge of the roof. She was pointing her revolver at Kate – so close that its nozzle was only an inch from her chest – and was forcing her, step by step, back towards the point where the roof ended, and the terrible drop began.

That wasn't the whole reason, though, for Kate's peculiar wail.

Barry was creeping up behind Bettina, and had almost reached her. Kate could see Barry over Bettina's shoulder – and was obviously doing her best to distract her attention, and drown the noise of his approaching footsteps.

Not that even Kate could keep up a wail for ever. Suddenly, she ran clean out of breath, and stopped, with a horrible choking groan.

'Keep walking, dear,' Bettina rasped. 'Just keep walking...'

Kate swallowed hard, and took one more backward step. It couldn't have been easy for her to do. Only one more step – and she'd be right at the edge of the roof...

As she took the backward step, Barry took a forward one. In under a second now, he'd be right behind Bettina. If only she didn't hear him, now that Kate was quiet...

Anne and Peter didn't move. They hardly dared to breathe. One sound from them, and Bettina might turn their way. And if she did, she'd be bound to see Barry...

At that moment, the worst possible thing happened. The door behind them crashed open, and loud footsteps sounded on the steps. Bettina couldn't fail to hear them. She started violently, and swung round – but saw nothing, for the simple reason that Barry was now close enough behind her to reach forward, and clap his hands over her eyes!

'Peek-a-boo, darling,' he murmured, in an imitation of her own husky voice. 'As I once said to my dear friend Humphrey Bogart...'

He broke off, as Bettina started struggling wildly, and shouted: 'Grab her gun, Kate – quick!'

Kate tried – but was suddenly knocked backwards by a vicious kick from Bettina. Backwards – to the very, very edge of the roof. She glanced round, had a dizzying glimpse of the whole town of Kettlewell swaying and swirling far beneath her, and drew back just in time. If her lungs or her throat could have stood it, she'd have screamed all over again. But all she could do was open and close her mouth like a fish.

Bettina, meanwhile, had succeeded in clawing Barry's hands away from her face. Barry was never at his best when fighting girls or women. Before he could stop her, she had shot away across the roof and was standing back against the chimney, that gun rock-steady in her hand.

'Curtain up on the grand finale!' she said theatrically. 'And I'm *so* sorry, dears – but I'm afraid it's curtain down for ever on the four of you . . .'

Her eyes blazed with such feverish intensity that it was as though they were sending out laser beams of hate.

'Down!' yelled Anne. 'Flat on your faces – everyone!'

It wouldn't do much good, she knew. There wasn't an inch of cover anywhere on that bleak, bare, totally flat roof. But it could make it just that little bit harder for Bettina to pick them off – and there were people on the stairs behind her: help was on its way.

In fact, that help was never needed.

As the Dean Street Detectives dropped to the ground, they heard three odd sounds from the direction of the chimney. A tinny clatter. A cry of pain. And the soft thud of a falling body. Barry was the first to pick himself up and go and see what had happened. And as a crowd of doctors, nurses and orderlies came charging up the steps from Ward A1, he was able to greet them with a calm announcement.

'I'm afraid Miss Bettina Rand has had an accident,' he said. 'A bit of chimney collapsed on top of her. I don't think she's seriously hurt.'

The poor boy must be half-hysterical, the doctors thought. It was almost as though he was about to burst out laughing . . .

A lot of things happened in the next hour or two.

Bettina Rand was taken on a stretcher to a private ward, where she speedily recovered consciousness – and was promptly arrested by Constable Anderson, who was, of course, no longer needed in the Intensive Care Unit. The constable was still a little doubtful about arresting such a great film star, but he had no choice, having taken statements from David Reynolds, the Dean Street Detectives, and just about everyone in Ward A1, including Detective Superintendent Miller.

The Detectives were made a great fuss of by the doctors, nurses, patients and visitors alike – but not by Mr Miller.

'I've not forgotten that you saved my life, and I'll always be grateful for that,' he grunted. 'But you also came darn close to giving me a seizure! I had to lie here completely helpless, listening to terrible noises from the roof and imagining the lot of you being killed a dozen times over.'

'Then it's just as well that *Twenty-First Century People* isn't being shown in our area,' the Detectives told him. 'Or you'd see us nearly being killed a dozen times more!'

They sounded so cheerful about it that Mr Miller finally grinned. 'Perhaps that's the whole trouble,' he said. 'Twenty-first century people are just too much for twentieth century fathers.'

'And mothers,' said Mrs Miller shakily.

The Dean Street Detectives were still trying to work out what to say to that when Mrs Miller stood up, and announced that it was time she took them home.

BILL BUTLER

The Spying Machines

'I hope you're right about those machines not seeing us. Because I've a nasty feeling that we've had it if they can!'

Is there any truth to the sinister rumours of deadly machines and a 'devil cat' passing through the streets of Fenton? The Dean Street Detectives investigate, and soon realise that in a race against time they alone can prevent a national disaster.

KNIGHT BOOKS

BILL BUTLER

The Fingers of Flame

'Boys – mostly skinheads, from the look of them – were suddenly appearing from all directions. In a split second, they'd emerged to surround the shed and leave the Dean Street Detectives completely trapped – four against forty, with just the bicycle racks and the bare wall behind them . . .'

Accused of vicious bullying, the Dean Street Detectives fall victim to a brutal kind of punishment from a gang of young thugs. But that's not the end of it. To their horror they find themselves being blamed for playing spiteful practical jokes and for deliberately starting fires. And NOBODY believes in their innocence . . .

KNIGHT BOOKS